Reminiscences of a Radar Plotter

Life in the Royal Navy in Ceylon at the end of World War 2.

by John Barford Lindop

First published privately 1989 as "A Sailor's Tale"
Revised and privately printed 1995
First published by Mercianotes 2015
Revised 2016

ISBN: 978-1-905999-24-8

© 1989 & 2016 John Barford Lindop

Published by:
Mercianotes
Wigton
CA7 5AQ
United Kingdom

enquiries@mercianotes.com
www.mercianotes.com

Contents

Preface

After about ten years of research the first edition of this history was completed in 1989 and subsequent to this various other material has surfaced that is of vital importance.

In particular a set of photographs relating to HMS Dabchick.

As a consequence of this long arm of co-incidence one is tempted to wonder just what other treasures may be out there somewhere and awaiting discovery.

As well as incorporating this new material sundry errors have been corrected and other odds and ends added including the resolving of the knotty problem of the Warrant Officer.

Hopefully this history is now, as was originally intended, a complete and accurate history of RN service with photos of every ship and shore bases served in.

Duddon, Tarporley, 1995.

Introduction

The mechanism whereby this *Magnus Opus* came into being was a combination of two factors, the first having just completed the Lindop family history, commenced in 1962, then looking for something to research next; factor two was a providential visit to the WW2 cruiser HMS Belfast moored on the Thames as a floating museum. Belfast was almost a twin to HMS Newcastle aboard which I sailed from the UK to Ceylon and this visit to HMS Belfast evoked instant and largely forgotten memories, awaking a nostalgia for events some forty years past; the research problems were immediately resolved, why not research Able Seaman Lindop and his service in the RN ?

Those looking for stories of Great Heroism and Able Seaman Lindop RP3 dodging shot and shell will be disappointed for the worst that befell me was a severe attack of singed eyebrows and hair due to playing Guy Fawkes and fooling about with disassembled Very Light cartridges. In fact, despite joining the RN to do my bit defending The British Way of Life and Democracy and to Fight European Fascism and Japanese Imperialism, which I interpreted as defending the British Empire, itself a product of British Imperialism and thus a bit of a political and philosophical conundrum, the only time enemy action got a bit too close was actually before joining up and therefore worthy of a mention.

This enemy action was, of course, visits by the Luftwaffe and between 29th October 1940 and 25th October 1941 there were ten raids on Chester City and a good deal more close by in the County. Raids on Chester resulted in the dropping of three parachute mines, forty four High Explosive bombs of varying sizes and three hundred and forty four 1-kilogram incendiary bombs, killing four and wounding fifteen. One hundred and seventy houses were damaged as well as the Gas Works, Sewage Works, Canal banks and the usual sundry damages to telephone lines, roads and general infrastructure.

On 28th October 1940, coinciding with a heavy attack on Liverpool and Birkenhead Docks parachute mines shattered nearly every pane of glass in Chester, Krystal Nacht with a vengeance.

The night of 7th April 1941 four H/Es, one delayed action and sixty five incendiaries fell on Queen's Park where we lived at the time; one incendiary failed to burn so I dug it out the following morning and it sits, suitably polished, on the desk as I write, a silent memorial to those stirring times. One bomb landed in the field at the side of the house but no-one heard it due to our being hidden away in the air raid shelter in the garage.

In the morning, surprise, surprise, a large hole in the ground tho' no damage was caused at all, not even a broken window.

Granny Lindop, just up the road and recently widowed, was not so lucky as a large bomb landed alongside her house causing considerable damage and a similar thing happened to wifey's granny as well; odd to relate all the bombs that fell on Queen's Park landed in gardens or open spaces and the unexploded one,

2nd October, 1944

TO: THE CHIEF CONSTABLE

Sir,

I respectfully beg to report that the following are brief details of the effects of bombing on this City :-

Date Raid Commenced	Type of Bombs and Number	Place	Casualties Civilian K. Serious Slight		C.D. Personnel K. Serious Slight			Damage
29. 8. 40	Incendiary Bombs 9	City Hospital, Station Rd. Oulton Place.						No fires requiring Fire Service.
25. 9. 40	H. E. 1	Field near Blacon School.						No damage.
25.10. 40	Incendiary 19	Handbridge area.						Slight damage to roof of one house.
18.11. 40	H.E. 3	Highfield Rd. Blacon.						Slight damage to residential property.
28.11. 40	21 H.E. 2 Para. Mines 188 I.B.	See reports by Chief Constable and Chief Officer, Fire Service.	2	2	4	1	1 1	Gas Works slightly damaged.
1. 1. 41	H.E. 1	Crane Street Adjacent Gas Works.	1	2	3			3 houses demolished, none damaged beyond repair but 15 seriously damaged.
7. 4. 41	3 H.E.,(1 U.X.) 65 I.B.	Queens Park area.	1					Casualty was a woman in Seaville Street injured by A.A. Shell. 29 Houses seriously damaged including a Wardens' Post. 90 slightly damaged. Electricity supply interrupted
15. 4..41.	11 H.E., 83 I.B's.	Roodee Racecourse.						Damage very slight.
22.10. 41	4 H.E.	Sewage Works, Sealand Road.			1			24" Main, 36" Main and 2 Settling Tanks damaged.
25.10. 41	1 Para. Mine	Shropshire Union Canal, Parkgate Rd.						30 houses damaged, Canal Bank damaged, Telephone wires cut.
TOTAL:	3 Para. Mines,44 H.E. 344 I.B's.		3	5	7 1		2 1	

Number of "Alerts" 232   Duration 383 hours 22 minutes

dud or delayed action, fell in Dutton's Nurseries, now built over, which we observed being excavated and steamed out the following morning and a whopper it was too, probably a 550-lb SC250.

The purpose of these raids remains unclear, they all coincided with raids on Merseyside and most probably they were the result of bombers dumping loads for whatever reason or opportunist bombing by those unable to find Merseyside, possibly confused by the Dee and Mersey estuaries and the decoy fires on the former, a problem today never mind in a medium bomber in the dark, in poor weather, with no radio aids and being shot at as well plus balloons and night fighters.

An enduring memory is the hollow bang of the anti-aircraft fire, the uneven, jinked hum of the aircraft engines and shrapnel whirring down all around, a considerably greater risk than the bombs.

These bombers, mainly He 111 and Ju 88s, were from Luftflotte 3 commanded by Generalfeldmarschall Sperrle based on newly captured airfields in France and caused consternation to the authorities by flying up the Irish Sea to Anglesea and then turning inland to their targets rather than the alternative over-land routes planned for them by the UK military and thereby very unsportingly rendering those defences largely impotent.

Nevertheless, some damage was inflicted on the attackers and two ended up crashing close to Chester, one a Ju 88 A5 from IV/Kg 3 crashed at Poulton killing all the crew and from which we salvaged, in true schoolboy fashion, sundry treasures, including bits of the crew; also a He 111P of KG 27 based at Rennes in Northern France attacked RAF Sealand and was imprudent enough to circle far more times than was good for it and was promptly shot down by Spitfire instructors from RAF Hawarden a few miles away across the Dee.

The machine crash landed in a field belonging to Border House Farm in Bumpers Lane and close to the Dee Marshes where Liverpool Decoy was sited, a fire site code named Star Fish depicting that city under attack and thereby deflecting raids, quite successfully it seems. The crew were invited to return to inspect the site a couple of years ago and it turns out they were the only complete crew to survive the war, an ill wind indeed.

Anyway, those who study the pages of history will know that the books are full of the names of Great Men and the Annals of War filled with Heroes;of those who took part in WW2 most will recall the top political figures, Hitler, Mussolini, Churchill, Stalin, Roosevelt; of the Heroes they will recall the names of the senior commanders such as Rommel, Patton, Eisenhower, Donitz, Zukov, Montgomery, *et al*; on a lesser scale were the products of press propaganda to feed a public need for Heroes, much practiced by the Germans and Americans and, to a lesser extent,by ourselves.

Various names peep out from the pages of history, Skorzeny of the SS, Bader of the RAF, Galland of the Luftwaffe. However, the Armed Forces numbered many millions of personnel, way beyond the level of everyday experience and understanding so, to narrow it down a bit,the RN had at its zenith some 855,000 personnel in June 1945, *i.e*: 783,000 men and 72,000 WRNS. If you deduct the Heroes it leaves an awful lot who do not appear in the history books; who did the driving, cooking, typing, manned the guns, operated the radios and radar; who did the coding, supply, fired the torpedoes; history hardly records them.

They were the vast anonymous mass of civilians, hastily put into service dress and even more hastily trained; called to perform their allotted tasks, then, when war passed by, slipped back into history again leaving little or no mark to record their passing.

As I type these pages many faces peer mistily through the keys, mostly their names have long since vanished, many will have now passed on to that great RN in the skies and the others dispersed to the four corners of the world; of the dozens, scores, perhaps hundreds of Jolly Jack Tars met whilst in the RN only a scanty handful can now be traced.

Of the ships served upon all have gone to the breakers years ago; many of the shore bases have gone the same way; St. Budeaux Camp, a part of HMS Impregnable, now a new housing estate,Vicarage Road Camp under a new road, Valkyrie has reverted to the hotels from which it sprang and Mayina dismantled with the site housing a university; all is not lost however, Drake is still alive and kicking, more or less the centre of RN activity now as Chatham and Portsmouth are closed; Bambara is the home of the small Sri Lanka Airforce; Collingwood is still there and houses the radar museum but Royal Arthur and Glendower have gone back to their old jobs as holiday camps tho' the latter still looks much the same from the road, and, indeed, on a recent visit it was evident that some 95% of the old Glendower is still there with its ghosts.

Even tracing the names of some of the ships was a problem; HMS Isle of Sark, the name of which was completely forgotten gradually emerged from the mists thanks to a great deal of sleuthing and the good offices of Miss Thirkettle from the Ministry of Defence (RN Historical Section) and ex Lt. Cdr. C.E. Turner RNVR the 1st Lieut. who sent some super photos including those taken of Divisions on the day he left the ship; incredibly one depicts myself,unknown at the time and it has taken all these years to get here.

A similar problem was HMS Dabchick and here memory played its usual tricks in that she was thought to be HMS Ladybird and thus the search floundered up many blind alleys tho' in the fullness of time and after endless adverts and letters she emerged correctly named.

In similar vein to HMS Isle of Sark someone aboard HMS Dabchick had taken photos but attempts to obtain a set met with a blank at the time as I left the ship before they became available and, over the years,the search was terminated as an unattainable dream.

Forty nine years later, replying to an advert in *RN Shipmates*, a Services contact newsletter, from an ex Dabchick Stoker, a set of photos arrived in reply;incredibly the set I was looking for all those years ago;even more incredibly I appear on one of them as will be seen, looking substantially younger and a ghost from the past indeed.

For the only known surviving private photograph of HMFDT-13 all of us are indebted to the ex 1st.Lieut.,Lt. Cdr. S. Burnaby Davies, RN (Ret) and a fine photos it is too even if she does look tatty and unloved in the evening of her life in the Graving Dock at Poplar after the end of our commission.

For a great deal of information concerning life aboard that I had forgotten until prompted I am indebted to ex shipmate Bill Bradshaw, also an RP3 from all those years ago.

Collecting for this history has required hundreds of letters all over the world, old shipmates have reappeared who I never thought I would hear from again and many correspondence friendships have been set up that are valued most highly, not only ex RN, but RAF, WAAF, WRNS and civvy boffins as well.

Research can take you down some strange roads; whilst twiddling the knobs of the radar sets I was operating there was always the strange notion that, somewhere, there was an opposite number in the Kriegsmarine doing the same thing and wondering what his opposite number in the RN might be doing and, in the search for this still elusive chap, Heinz Guske appeared on the scene, ex P.O. Funker on U 764 who filled in the gaps relating to radio and radar and life in the Kriegsmarine in so far as it affected U Boats.

Many others have ably assisted; the IWM, PRO, NMM, Ministry of Defence (RN), Dick Imrie, Peter Cole, Peter Gates to name but a few.

Looking back on it all I wouldn't have missed it for anything, for, straight from school,the misty daydreams of the Wizard and Rover had come to life and for one with a decided technical bent and a vast interest in guns, ships, aeroplanes and anything mechanical it was too good to be true. What thoughts would have been engendered had I been obliged to see my shipmates drowning or trapped in a blazing ship I would not care to hazard a guess.

However this work is compiled, not as an exercise in deering do, but largely as a social history for those in the future who might wonder what at least one of the great legion of nobodies did during WW2.

As for those who did not return from the conflict, and some 264,443 did not, including 50,758 RN personnel; today it would be a hard job to explain just what they sacrificed their lives for.

After two generations of the most horrendous bloodletting, our racial cousins, the Germans, now have the strongest economy in Europe and are among our closest allies.

The Japanese, once sneered at as a bunch of mediaeval farmers, came close to beating us at our own game and, if it had not been for the USA and Russia, would have done so; today they have the world's most successful economy owning large parts, in industrial terms, of their old enemies, the USA and UK. One must be forgiven for thinking that the sacrifices seem to have been in vain, it certainly looks a bit that way.

Duddon, Tarporley, 1989

The Groves, Chester.

Part 1

Before Bambara

Early Days

Earliest Rig of the Day seems to have been a Shantung Buster Suit and when I outgrew this it was replaced with a sailors' suit complete with a ratings style cap; this was the late twenties and early thirties and a popular garb, both here and around the world generally.

There was no particular interest at home in things naval other than the fact that Britain was a trading nation depending on a large merchant navy to carry this out, plus being an island with the sea within easy reach from most points.

Introduction to boats came soon enough as the family lived in Chester close to the river Dee with its varied selection of craft available for hire for a modest fee as well as motor launches, the crews of which wore smart naval-type uniforms, that ran trips up the river as far as Eaton Hall, the home of the Duke of Westminster; my earliest boating memories are of those trips complete with picnics and, I suppose, suitably dressed in the appropriate sailor suit.

The first experience on a ship of any substance was on the occasion of the annual visit to Liverpool; this was effected either by rail to Rockferry and thence to Liverpool via the underground electric railway or bus/rail to Birkenhead

Hinderton.

Woodside and catch the Mersey Ferry at ld a go, the Queensway Tunnel still in the future.

Trips to Liverpool afforded the opportunity of a tram ride, usually the high point of the visit, Chester's trams having been scrapped in 1930; in fact Mother's Father, 'Pop' John Worral, had been the last General Manager of the Birkenhead United Tramways & Omnibus Company so perhaps it was catching.

HMS Norfolk.

A memory firmly engraved on my mind is standing on the upper deck of the ferry, probably *Hinderton*, and watching the landing stage receding from us in a somewhat eerie manner.

Each year the family holidays were at Prestatyn; a house was booked for a few weeks from one Miss Hawkins, a shadowy figure dressed in black who lived in Highbury Avenue close to the shore, it was all Percy Pickles, Pierrots and toast rack busses and the sun seemed to shine most of the time.

It was discovered that there was a battleship tied up at Llandudno and visitors were welcome, the RN was 'showing the flag' so off we trooped, complete with a brand new specially purchased double barreled pop gun as seemed appropriate to this military occasion.

The battleship, tied up at the pier, was actually a cruiser, *HMS Norfolk*, later to be deeply involved in mutiny tho' no sign was apparent, no corpses hanging

S.S. St. Tudno.

from the yardarms tho' I was to suffer, up to that point, one of life's total humiliations (there were far worse to come) when one of the crew passed a remark about my popgun; funny how you remember seemingly trivial incidents.

Not long after there was more ship time, actually real sea time itself on a real ship; this was aboard *SS St.Tudno* of the Liverpool and North Wales Steamship Company which ran, among other routes, trips along the North Wales coast, usually from Llandudno to Menai and back so Mother, Aunt Muriel and myself, suitably dressed, not in a sailor suit, but the finest Harris Tweed plus cap partook of such a trip.

St.Tudno is long gone but had an interesting career; built by Fairfields in 1926 and thus the same age as myself, she displaced some 2,326 tons and, like most ships taken over by the RN during WW2 for conversion, in this case, into an Armed Boarding Vessel. Part of the conversion was suitable armament, including a large gun on the after deck but without sufficient homework being done on the load carrying capabilities for, when the gun was fired, the whole lot collapsed through the deck doing a great deal of damage; there must have been some very red faces. She was repaired and, presumably, a gun of more modest dimensions fitted for next she appears as a Minesweeping Depot Ship until demob., finally to be scrapped at Ghent in 1963 after a career spanning some thirty seven years. About this time was the first and only meeting with Uncle Charles; he was a Captain

Uncle Charles.

for Elders and Ffyfes and did the banana run between the UK and Fernando Poo, and, in fact, died at sea after the war.

He was the family connection with the sea and, in some insidious way, must have influenced my later thinking, but at the time he remained a shadowy figure; clearly the seeds were sown but remained dormant for some considerable time.

After this encouraging naval start things turned to aeroplanes, to become the main interest in life and all thoughts of ships disappeared.

The first flight was off the roof of the garden shed, recently purchased for passing the entrance exams for the King's School in Chester; this embryonic

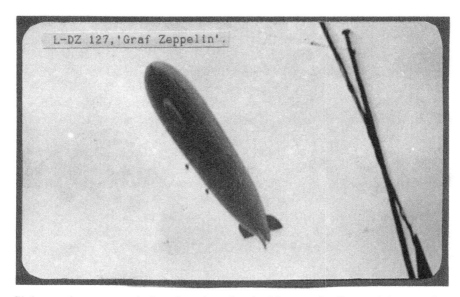

L-DZ 127,'Graf Zeppelin'.

flight was into our sand play pit and, assisted with an umbrella, straight onto the sharp edge of a spade so blood everywhere and a scar to this day; it was clear that flight theory required some rethinking.

Not long after this abortive effort an airship, one of the wonders of the age, Graf Zeppelin D-LZ 127, flew over the house at about a thousand feet; it was a Sunday morning and Father rushed out and took a photograph with the family Brownie Box Camera; I can still hear the roar of the engines and it established aviation even more for me.

The first flight was in a DH Dragon complete with wicker-work seats from Hooton Park about 1934, more than likely a five-shilling flip and this aviation activity turned out to be a takeoff, flight North along the Mersey parallel with the runway and then landing.

There was an entrancing view of the Mersey and an even more entrancing view through the gaps in the laced up fabric of the fuselage; I did not know then just how significant it all was.

The nineteen thirties rolled rapidly by accompanied by the

Alan Bennett.

increasingly strident demands of Chancellor Hitler whilst acres of black and brown uniformed steel-helmeted and jackbooted legions stamped their way across Germany and, later, most of Europe.

Talk of war was everywhere, Chamberlains nettle danger stung him badly and he faded from the pages of history heaped with odium.

My birthday was September 3rd., 1939, Father came into the garden and announced that, once again, we were at war with Germany; what mysterious forces were at work guiding my subconscious ?

My friend Alan Bennett had joined the Merchant Navy as a Cadet Deck Officer and came home on leave in a resplendent uniform with tales of great heroics dodging Stuka dive bombers on the Malta convoys, trips to New York and the like, it must have made an impression.

Uncle Charles gave up the bananas and became Lt. C.R. Hodder R.N.R. taking up his Commission in the RN Reserve to which he had belonged for many years as did many Merchant Navy personnel, forming a highly skilled reserve for wartime emergencies.

From 1941 onwards he was aboard *HMS Ariguani*, originally a banana ship of Elders & Ffyfes displacing 6,746 tons and built in 1926 ; she was requisitioned by the RN for conversion into an Ocean Boarding Vessel and later into a Fighter Catapult Ship, this latter, in default of suitable aircraft carriers,was a somewhat desperate stopgap measure in an attempt to counter the FW Kondor long range aircraft of the Luftwaffe which were wreaking havoc on our convoys and passing siting reports to the U Boats. Hurricane fighter aircraft were launched from a catapult some seventy feet long built on the fore part of the hull and launching over the bows via a rocket propelled sledge; if the aircraft were not shot down and could not make it to land they were obliged to land on the water and hope to be picked up.

HMS Ariguani was disabled by a T5 Accoustic torpedo on a homebound convoy from Gibraltar; she docked there for copious patching of the stern with wooden plating and then towed home to Greenock in 1943 with Uncle Charles as Commanding Officer.

Final influences were at Wrekin College where I was at school;senior members left to join the various forces,many of them to reappear in due course in the uniform of the RN, several of them as pilots in the Fleet Air Arm, the die was cast.

Volunteering

By now it was clear that the plan would be to join the RN with a view to becoming a pilot in the Fleet Air Arm, thus satisfying all interests in one fell swoop so the address of the relevant Naval recruiting office was obtained from a schoolmate and a letter duly sent off offering my services to His Majesty.

In the fullness of time the expected official looking brown envelope arrived requesting the pleasure of a visit to the RN Selection Centre located at 13/15, Nantwich Road, Crewe whereby interviews, medicals and sundry selections would be made.

Uncle Horace Lindop, a bank manager, lived just down the road from the Centre so opportunity was taken of his generous invitation to stay for the purpose of the Selection, eventually to present myself for inspection by their Lordships, or representatives thereof.

In my pocket was a letter of commendation from the Commanding Officer of 540 Squadron ATC, indicating, in his opinion that I was of suitable educational standard and had, in addition, a substantial grounding in things military, having previously been in the school Officer Training College and currently in the Air Training Corps (ATC). The Air Training Corps was one of the wonders of the age and thus worthy of some comment with regard to the history and organisation.

The origins of the ATC were founded on the previous Air Defence Cadet Force (ADCF) which had been formed in July 1938 as a direct counter to the growing might of the Luftwaffe and within a very short time grew to a considerable size. In February 1941 the authorities deemed that, for reasons best known to themselves, a new body was required and formed the Air Training Corps incorporating the Air Defence Cadet Force; the Air Training Corps followed the Air Defence Cadet Force and RAF structure of Flights, Squadrons and so forth and had an RAF-style uniform, in fact that of the ADCC with a change of buttons and badges.

Due to a great deal of propaganda relating to the German aviation threat and a vast amount of lobbying of schools and such bodies the ATC grew to a formidable size and within a few months some 200,000 young men were enrolled; it was some 25% of all the young men in Britain aged between 16 and 18 and a staggering piece of organisation.

This was starting to put into effect the stated intention of winning the war through overwhelming air power and a threat that came to a terrible fruition, devastating Germany from end to end.

In all some half a million joined the Air Training Corps up to VJ Day; of those some 170,000 joined the armed services, 100,000 joined the RAF and half of those went for aircrew, a vital contribution to the war effort.

Squadron 540 was formed at Wrekin College in September 1941 thus I was one of the first ATC Cadets.

R.N. Recruiting Centre, Crewe.

Meanwhile.... back at the RN Recruiting/Selection Centre in Crewe there was a stiff medical and endless questionnaires of sundry sorts to assess educational and intellectual standards.

Suitably completed it was time for The Interview and this was conducted by a Captain RN and two Lesser Persons, a Lieutenant on one side and a S/Lt. pilot on the other, plus a model aircraft carrier on the baize covered table.

My letter of commendation was read without comment, "Why did I want to join the RN, had I any relatives in the service?" and all that sort of thing. The Fleet Air Arm (FAA) representative asked some technical questions relating to the use of carriers by aircraft, which way did the ship steam to fly on and off, what did I know about things mechanical and aeroplanes in particular.

The Interview was over and a decision would be available shortly.

In due course I was ushered back into The Presences; they regretted that there were no vacancies for me as a pilot in the FAA but as I was obviously keen on flying why did I not try for the RAF as they were crying out for aircrew?

Having thus been turned down as a naval pilot was a blow tho' it was not revealed if I personally had flopped or there really was a considerable surplus of FAA pilots; in retrospect this was found, at least in part, to be the case and the RN had trained more pilots than the actual losses demanded and that these underemployed chaps were sweeping out the hangars for something to do, or so said the sailors tales.

This exotic spectacle was never seen but illustrated the point admirably. From that comment it was more than clear that crunch time had arrived; as Oswald Mosley had noted in his

A.T.C Cadet Lindop.

famous speech at Olympia "the moment of truth, the moment of destiny" and it was on me at that instant.

The chances of surviving the war would now depend on the next split second decision; what the Interviewer had not mentioned about the RAF was the fact that the shortage of aircrew was due to the losses occasioned by the bombing campaign over Germany, the fields of Europe were littered with the burnt out wrecks of Bomber Command and horrendous casualty lists disfigured the Press; was I to be numbered among these?

It was clear that this was not the way to survive so, despite failing to get to FAA pilot, the possibility of joining the RN proper was raised in some, as yet, unidentified guise.

They beamed with pleasure at this very sensible request to join them in the Senior Service, mainly brought about by a strong feeling of self preservation; would I sign here please? And I was in the RN.

On the way out someone handed over a small naval type badge in the usual red cotton on navy background, a naval crown in the centre and the letters RNYE disposed in each corner; this was the badge of the RN Youth Entry for attachment to my ATC uniform; it was given without comment and I supposed that all volunteers were given such a badge and thought nothing more of it. Nearly forty years later, as a consequence of research for this work, it was discovered that the RN Youth Scheme was not as I had originally thought but a Selection process for potential officers and obtaining a copy of a book entitled The Navy and the Y Scheme told all, some forty years too late alas.

At the time of joining none of the literature mentioned it and no-one had thought to observe that I was attempting to join via the Y Scheme never mind what it was all about.

Most of the book reads like extracts from Ripping Yarns and The Boys Own Paper, no mention of drowning in a depth-charged submarine, blown to bits in a Motor Torpedo Boat (MTB) or choking to death in fuel oil from a torpedoed battleship.

The bones of the Y Scheme were as follows:

The object of the Scheme is threefold:

1, to pick out in advance young men considered likely to do well in the Navy.

2, to enable them to get into the Service of their choice and

3, until they are old enough to be called up they must receive suitable pre-military training in one of the recognised units, *i.e*: Home Guard, Sea Cadets, Army Cadets, Air Training Corps (ATC) and so on.

To be accepted into the Y Scheme means that he is a marked man and has, during his service training, every opportunity to prove himself worthy of a Commission.

Well, it is nice to know even after all this time tho' being a marked man could not have been all that apparent, however it did mean that I joined the Service of choice and didn't end up in the Army or down the mines as a Bevin Boy, a daunting thought indeed.

Unbeknown to myself, I was now a Y Scheme Entry for the RN and, stitching the badge onto the ATC uniform, continued with training.

By this time flying experience flights had been fixed up with RAF Shawbury and flying was undertaken in Wellington 13s of the Central Navigation School.

The first flight in a Wellington was quite interesting if slightly unnerving as the Geodetic construction made for great flexibility and watching the wings wave all over the place made one consider the general safety of the machine tho' it was immensely strong.

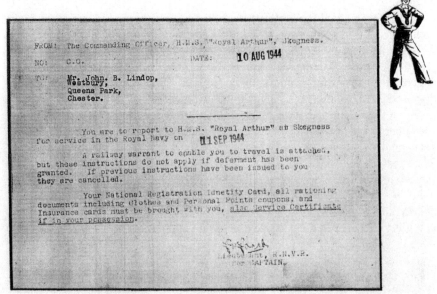

FROM: The Commanding Officer, H.M.S. "Royal Arthur", Skegness.

NO: C.O. DATE: **10 AUG 1944**

TO: Mr. John. B. Lindop,
Westbury,
Queens Park,
Chester.

You are to report to H.M.S. "Royal Arthur" at Skegness for service in the Royal Navy on **1 SEP 1944**

A railway warrant to enable you to travel is attached, but these instructions do not apply if deferment has been granted. If previous instructions have been issued to you they are cancelled.

Your National Registration Idnetity Card, all rationing documents including Clothes and Personal Points coupons, and Insurance cards must be brought with you, also Service Certificate if in your possession.

LIEUTENANT, R.N.V.R.
for CAPTAIN.

A few weeks later D-Day came with Operations Neptune and Overlord whilst we got ourselves prepared for School Certificate Examinations, due towards the end of school year in July.

The end of term came up rapidly and with the School Certificate exams completed and passed the ATC contingent left for summer camp at RAF Honiley where we were accommodated with a London ATC Squadron.

There was very intensive training in all RAF disciplines on this very active field with arms drill, shooting on the range, parachute packing, runs on the bomb aimer and flying in an Airspeed Oxford.

From Honiley I returned home for good having left school, the ATC uniform was packed up and sent back to the Squadron and all that could be done was hang around and wait.

By now it was August 1944 and no-one could anticipate the effects of Operations Neptune and Overlord, the Allies might well be repulsed and the situation regarding Japan was regarded with grave foreboding considering the formidable fighting capabilities of their armed forces.

My 18th birthday was on September 3rd and it was clear that the call up notice would arrive any day, I knew very little about ships, less about the Royal Navy and had scant idea as to what my role might be when the call came. I was to find out soon enough as the call up papers arrived dated August 10th advising that "You are to report to HMS Royal Arthur at Skegness for service in the Royal Navy on September 11th", just eight days after my birthday, obviously the system worked only too well.

A Rail Warrant was enclosed, a cold hand reached out and gripped me tight.

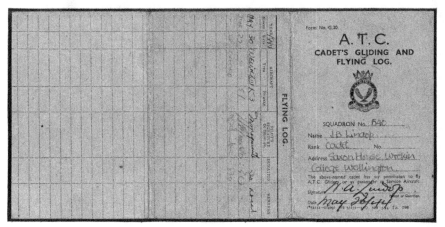

HMS Royal Arthur

Or, How I Joined the Royal Navy and Saw the World.

Clutching a Travel Warrant and scant bits and pieces I joined the Skegness train at Chester Station on the morning of September 11th 1944; of those boarding the train many were recognised as from around the town as friends or schoolmates and clearly on a similar mission.

Groups of parents stood around to see them off, most likely those parents had done their bit in WW1 and one could only guess at their thoughts now seeing their sons off to fight in yet another war, one they had done so much to try to prevent.

At Skegness station the party was met by an elderly Petty Officer, dressed in what appeared to be the livery of one of the railway companies and he herded us into lorries in a curt and hectoring manner and off we went to *HMS Royal Arthur*.

Driving through the main gate it was immediately apparent that this establishment had once been a holiday camp in happier times, one of Billy Butlin's in fact and over the main gate, in an arch of carefully wrought iron was the legend 'Our True Intent is all for Your Delight' but this brought little response as, with dry mouths and butterfly stomachs, most of us were lost in our own thoughts.

This *Royal Arthur* had been commissioned in 1939 and remained in use by the RN until 1946; there had been a previous use of the name in the 7,700 ton cruiser launched in 1893 and named after Prince Arthur the Duke of Connaught, one of the sons of Queen Victoria.

How many recruits arrived with me can no longer be recalled but we were split into classes of fifty, mine being Class 274 in the charge of an old salt, one Leading Seaman Goddard, identified as such by the anchor on his left sleeve; he was the Class Killick, RN slang for Leading Seaman derived from the Celtic word for an anchor.

Identity Cards and Rations Books were handed in and a meal obtained in Kent House, the same as for the jolly campers, in fact many of the holiday camp decorations were still in place.

Chalets were allocated for the night and I teamed up with Joe Lewis from a similar background to myself.

One of the few benefits of having been to boarding school then became apparent for the psychological problems of having been dragged from a stable home environment into a turmoil like *Royal Arthur* was quite traumatic for those who had never been away from home before and there must have been some acute cases of homesickness.

For my own part all these problems had been resolved years before and thus was able to stand on my own two feet and easily weather whatever storm might come my way.

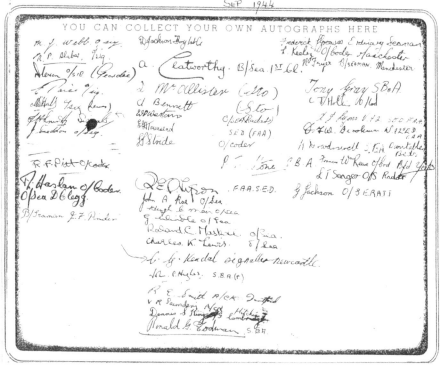

The following day induction proper started, *Royal Arthur* seemed to be a seething cauldron of activity, endless columns of men in naval attire doubling everywhere, the parade ground full of classes being drilled and harangued; one of the first decisions was what trade branch to join bearing in mind what was available.

Of those on offer Cooks, Writers, Supply and Radar spring to mind tho' there may well have been others, so with a decided technical bent and an interest in radio, I put my name down to be trained as a radar operator but with little idea of what was entailed as radar was one of the Great Secrets of the war.

Induction into the RN was notable for joining queues for almost everything; photographs, pay books, food, medicals, innoculations, psychological tests, haircuts and, a couple of days later, an issue of uniforms and kit; in this latter case we stood in line in the Clothing stores while some busy Wrns Supply ratings took an accurate look at us all and a hail of clothing and gear came flying across the counter, almost all fitting first time. The kit list of an Ordinary Seaman was formidable and a very large kit bag was required to hold it all; in addition there was a hammock and bedding, it all cost the taxpayers a resounding £12 15s 6d (£12.78) or thereabouts.

I can still smell the coarse blue serge material today as we struggled to find out what went where with the sailors collars, silks, lanyards, flapped trousers, tight fitting jumpers and the general dearth of pockets.

S.—98 (Established April, 1923).
(Revised May, 1943).

KIT LIST

MEN DRESSED AS SEAMEN

O.N. ?X540875

Name.... LINDOOP. JOHN.B.   Rating.... AB. (HO)

Reg. Kit	Item	Dates	15/10	17/1/47	15/11/47							
2	Serge Jumpers		3	3	3							
2	Prs. Serge Trousers		3	3	3							
‡2	Duck or Drill Jumpers		2	2	2							
*2	Prs. Duck or Drill Trousers		2	2	2							
†1	Blue Overall Suit (2 for Stokers and Air Mechanics) ...		—	—	—							
1	Pr. Fearnought Trousers (Stokers in coal fired ships only) ...		—	—	—							
2	Blue Jean Collars		4	4	5							
2	Caps, Blue or White		2	2	2							
2	Cap Ribbons (See A.F.O. 750/44)		3	2	2							
1	B.S. Scarf		2	2	2							
2	Prs. Socks or Stockings (2 prs. Socks to new entries)		9	7	8							
2	,, Boots (or 1 pr. Boots and 1 pr. black leather Shoes: 2 prs. Boots to new entries)		5	3	3							
1	Bed		1	1	1							
1	Blanket		1	1	2							
2	Bed Covers		2	2	2							
2	Cotton Flannels		4	4	5							
2	Singlets		5	5	3							
1	Jersey		2	2	2							
1	Knife (Seamen branch ratings and wiremen ; optional for others) ...		1	—	1							
1	,, Lanyard		1	1	1							
1	Soap Bag		1	1	1							
1	Hair Comb		3	4	1							
1	,, Brush		N.I.	—	1							
1	Tooth ,, ...		1	1	1							
1	Hard Boot Brush		1	1	1							
1	Polishing Boot Brush		1	1	1							
1	Type		1	1	1							
1	Attache Case		1	2	1							
2	Prs. Drawers		7	7	4							
2	Towels		5	5	7							
1	Waistbelt, blue		1	1	1							
1	Oilskin Coat (Optional on the China and East Indies Station) ...		1	1								
—	Badges as necessary		✓	✓	✓							
1	Vol. I. Seamanship Manual (O.S. & Boys only)		—	—								
1	Stokers' Manual (Stokers only)		—	—								
1	Signal Card (Signal Ratings only)		—	—								
‡2	Hammocks		2	2	2							
‡1	Set Clews		1	1								
‡1	Lashing		1	1	1							
‡1	Kit Bag		1	1	1							

‡ Government property.

† The working dress in submarines for seaman, telegraphist, signal and stoker ratings is the blue overall suit. While serving *at home* three blue overall suits are to be provided by seaman, telegraphist, signal and stoker ratings as compulsory kit.

* Not to be issued to naval Airmen under training as pilots or observers.

Sta. 10094/43

Heavy boots, gas masks, gaiters and so on all found their place on our bodies and thus kitted-out we attended the first Divisions in the RN, to be revealed as morning parade where we doubled past the Captain puffing and panting in our gas masks and then on to endless drill and lectures.

One of the latter was a harangue by the Camp Padre, stern talk about the use of foul language and Christian conduct.

After a few weeks being knocked into shape shore leave was granted to visit the delights of 'Skeggy' in wartime and this led to my first brush with Those in Authority.

Reg. Kit	Optional Articles	Dates	16/10	17/1	5/11/46					
1	Overcoat ...		1.	1	1					
1	Oilskin, sou' wester ...		—	—	—					
1	Serge Jumper } (On Home Station only)		1.	1	1					
1	Pr. Serge Trousers		1.	1	1					
1	Jumper, duck or drill		—1.	—	—					
1	Pr. Trousers, duck or drill		—1.	—	—					
1	Pr. White Shoes ... (On Foreign Station only)		—	—	—					
2	Prs. White Socks ...		—	1	1					
1	Waistbelt, white ...		1.	1	1					
1	Pr. Boots, Sea, rubber (Seamen and signal ratings serving in sea-going ships only)		—	—	—					
1	Pr. Black Leather Slippers ...		—	—	—					
2	Suits Pyjamas ...		2.	1	—					
1	Pr. Scissors ...		1.	2.	2					
1	Razor ...		1.	1	1					
1	Pr. Gloves, Woollen ...		—	—	—					
6	Pocket Handkerchiefs		14.	8	—					
1	Shaving Brush ...		—	—	1					
1	Clothes Brush ...		1.	1	1					
1	B.S. Scarf ...		1.	1	1					
1	Housewife ...		—	—	1					
2	Cholera Belts ...		—	—	—					
1	Comforter, blue ...		—	1	1					
1	Scarf, plain white ...		—.	1	1					
1	Pillow ...		—	—	—					
2	Pillow Covers ...		—	2.	—					
1	Blanket (On Home Station only) ...		—	—	1					
1	Cap Box ...		—	—	—					

Divl. Officer .....
H.M.S. .....
Date .....

Divl. Officer .....
H.M.S. .....
Date .....

Divl. Officer .....
H.M.S. .....
Date .....

Divl. Officer .....
H.M.S. .....
Date .....

Divl. Officer .....
H.M.S. .....
Date .....

Divl. Officer .....
H.M.S. .....
Date .....

Divl. Officer .....
H.M.S. .....
Date .....

Divl. Officer .....
H.M.S. .....
Date .....

NOTE.—This form is to be kept by the Divisional Officer (K.R. & A.I. Article 1158a, clause 13). On a man leaving a Ship or Establishment the form is to be brought up to date and transferred with his other papers, i.e., placed with the Service Certificate, attached to Form S.47, or attached, with a duplicate copy, to Form S. 258, as appropriate.

(21559) 35498/Ds212 875,000 12/44 K.H.K. Gp. 8/8

Lined up outside the guardroom for leave inspection I was accosted by some person acting like a Petty Officer but attired in Officer type clothing, "Why was I badly shaven," bellowed this vision, "Clear off and get properly shaved", which of course was promptly acted upon.

I was to find that this oddity was called a Warrant Officer, a sort of half officer and half rating who dwelt in an in between world, neither one nor the other and treated as such by both those parties.

There was also a Commissioned Warrant Officer wearing what appeared to be a Sub-Lieutenant uniform but could easily be distinguished by age, manner and general agressiveness and to be avoided at all cost.

A 4 5 qr...... 63

If a copy of this Form is required,
Form S. 1243 is to be used.

S.—459 (Revised—August, 1939).

CERTIFICATE of the Service of

SURNAME (In Block Letters)	CHRISTIAN NAME OR NAMES
LINDOP	John Barford

in the Royal Navy.

NOTE—The corner of this certificate is to be cut off where indicated if the man is discharged with a "Bad" character or with disgrace, or if specially directed by the Admiralty. If the corner is cut off, the fact is to be noted in the Ledger.

Port Division — Devonport

Official No. — JX 540845

Date of Birth — 3rd September 1926

Where born { Town or Village — Chester
{ County — Cheshire

Trade or occupation on entry — Student

Religious Denomination — Church of England

Man's Signature on discharge to Pension

Wrexham

Nearest known Relative or Friend.
(To be noted in pencil.)

Relationship : FATHER

Name : WILLIAM ALFRED LINDOP

Address : WESTBURY.
QUEENS PARK
11/47 CHESTER. CHESHIRE

All Engagements, including Non-C.S., to be noted in these Columns.			Swimming Qualifications.		
Date of actually volunteering	Commencement of time	Period volunteered for	Date.	Qualification.	Signature.
1. 24 Apr HN	3 Sep 44	until the end of the period of the present emergency (VOLUNTEER)	1.		
2.			2.		
3.			3.		
4.			4.		
5.			5. S.IC... 085525		
6.			6.		

Medals, Clasps, &c., L.S. and G.C. Gratuity. (see also Page 4).

Date received or forfeited	Nature of Decoration	Date received or forfeited	Nature of Decoration
			LBAY 106 3

Description of Person	Stature		Chest, In.	Colour of			Marks, Wounds, and Scars
	Feet	In.		Hair	Eyes	Complexion	
On Entry as a Boy.........							
On advancement to man's rating, or on entry under 28 years......... On re-engagement or re-entry for C.S. or for Non-C.S. after attaining 28 years	5	6½	32¾	Brown Eagle	Hazel	Pale	abdominal scar R.
Further description if necessary							

CAUTION : This is an Official document. Any alteration made to it without proper authority, will render the offender liable to severe penalties.

N. 7863/38.

(1651) Wt. 17484/D7749 200M. 6/43 P.I. Gp. 740-62
S. 459.

2.

Name LINDOP John Banford

Name of Ship. (Tenders to be inserted in brackets)	Substantive Rating	Non-Substantive Rating	From	To	Cause of Discharge and other notations authorised by Article 606, Clause 9, K.R. and A.I.
Royal Arthur	Ord Sea		24 apl '44 Entry Routine	24 apl '44	Released to Reserve A.F.O. 2349/41
— " —	— " —		11 Sep. 44	23 Oct '44	
Glendower	Ord Sea		24 Oct 44	2 Mch '45	
Valkyrie	— " —		5 Mch '45	30 March '45	
Collingwood	— " —		31 Mch '45	20 Apl 45	
— " —	— " —	A/RP 3	21 apl 45	7 May 45	
Drake	— " —	— " —	8 May '45	14 July 45	
Drake IV (FDT 13)	— " — A/A.B.	— " —	15 July 45 11 Sept 45	16 Oct 45	
Drake	— " —	— " —	2 Oct 45	31 Dec '45	
Harpia	— " —	— " —	1 Jan. 46	31 Mar. 46	
Barabara (late Ausonia)	— " —		Apl. 46	6 May 46	
Barabara	— " —		7 May 46	26 Nov 47	
Drake	— " —		27 Nov 47	16 Mch '48	Released in Class A

Date	Wounds received in Action and Hurt Certificate ; also any meritorious Service, Special recommendations, Prize or other Grants ; temporary advancements to local (acting) ratings, with inclusive dates.	Captain's Signature
19 Dec 46	WG → PWG Credited NS 455160	Price

23

Name of Ship (Tenders to be inserted in brackets)	Substantive Rating	Non-Substantive Rating	From	To	Cause of Discharge and other notations authorised by Article 606, Clause 9, K.R. and A.I.

Examinations passed and Notations of Qualifications other than those entered on History Sheets ; also, for ratings of the Stoker Branch only, Qualifications affecting advancement.

Date	Particulars	Captain's Signature	Date	Particulars	Captain's Signature
3 Jan 45	Tr				
W.E.(P) 1/7/46	NIL				

4.

| Name | LINDOP | John Bamford | Conduct. |

Second Class for Conduct (inclusive dates)		Character and Efficiency on 31st December yearly, on final discharge, and other occasions prescribed by regulation. If qualified by service and recommended for Re-engagement or for Medal and Gratuity, "R.R." or "R.M.G." to be awarded on 31st December and final discharge, if not, a line to be drawn across column. Character is assessed as follows:—V.G., Good, Fair, Indifferent, Bad.
From	To	**Note as to method of assessing Efficiency.**

Superior—above average efficiency. } in substantive rating, held at
Satisfactory—average efficiency. } the time, without regard to
Moderate—less than average efficiency. } fitness for advancement.
Inferior—inefficient.

Variations in efficiency are often explained by the fact that the man had recently been promoted—see pages 2 and 3—and had not gained sufficient experience in his new position to justify a higher award than that actually assessed.

Good Conduct Badges			Character	Efficiency in Rating, noting substantive rating in brackets	Whether R.R. R.M.G. or not.	Date	Captain's Signature
Date	1st, 2nd, 3rd.	Granted, Deprived, Restored	V.G.	4. (Ord Sea)		31 DEC '44	Aus William
			VG	Sat' (H/AB)		31 Dec '45	R Simpson
			VG	Sat (A/AB)		31 DEC 46	E Prio
			VG	Sat (A/AB)		31 Dec 47	H Role Dutt
			VG	Sat (A/AB).	5/1	16 Feb '48	H Role a Dutt

Time forfeited					
Date	P., D., C., C.P., W.T.	Number of days			
		Awarded	Served		

25

HMS Royal Arthur was Commanded by Captain Rotherham RN with a support staff of some ninety officers heavily larded with doctors and dentists and an additional twenty two Wrn. Officers, plus some two hundred Wrn ratings who did all the usual Cooks, Writers, Supply and such jobs and they must have been run off their feet dealing with the throughput of trainees,some 260,000 in all during the war, some 30% of all RN wartime intake.

Among the Wrn. officers was 3rd. officer Phyllis Mary Lindop, met whilst doing some of the psychological and educational papers to assess fitness for radar training. Born in Cheltenham in 1916, Phyllis was from the Newport, Shropshire branch of the family and not directly related. By now properly inducted into the

Phyllis Mary Lindop

RN some considerable efforts were expended in getting everyone properly disciplined and inculcated with RN lore and conversant with King's Regulations and Admiralty Instructions which governed all our existence.

We learned that time in the RN was indicated by bells with appropriate noises and divided into watches, most were four hours but two were called Dog Watches of two hours, personnel were likewise divided into watches, or parts of ship to which all ship's company were allocated, port,starboard, red, green, foscle, foretop and so on.

Leave was 'going ashore', the floor was 'deck', ceiling was 'deckhead',walls were 'bulkheads', hospital was 'sick bay' and so on.

This system was operated by a hierarchy of Leading Seamen i.e. the mess, Petty Officers and then Divisional Officers; above them the Commander then Captain.

RA, as it was known, had suffered a bombing attack some time before our arrival, a fighter bomber had zipped in across the North Sea and caught everyone by surprise and caused some considerable damage so the place was very twitchy tho' fortunately there was no repeat.

The greatest hazard suffered was a widespread outbreak of enteritis, a condition notorious for its virulence and it seems that the whole of RA was affected for the pressure on the heads was more than they could reasonably accommodate and there were some unhappy sights in the mornings until the condition subsided.

Class 274 at HMS Royal Arthur

Of course there were the usual sailors tales of the Sick Bay being full to busting with those who could not cope, either physically or mentally, with the violent change in their style of living and suggestions that some considerable volume of unfortunates went out of the back door in the dead of night artfully smuggled away by the local undertakers, were most, if not all, the product of overactive imaginations.

The best that I could manage was,inexplicably,a bad attack of piles and thus excused drill for a bit until the gunge from the Sick Bay could do its stuff to exorcise the condition.

It looks as if the class had by now been knocked into some sort of disciplined unit after endless hours of drilling on the parade ground and countless lectures so most were considered fit for further training at a more specialised establishment.

At this point Class 274 contained several trades; Cooks,Writers, Supply etc. who wore 'fore and aft rig', i.e: jackets, trousers and peaked caps and were referred to as 'taxi drivers'; us proper sailors wore 'square rig' with the traditional 19th. century bell bottom trousers, jean collars, sailors caps and were known as 'men dressed as milk churns'.

It was then learned that our basic trade would be that of Seaman and the trade of radar operator was called a Non Substantive Rate and would follow Seaman training; there were two possibilities here, one was at *HMS Raleigh* and the other at *HMS Glendower*, the latter well known for being in the wilds of Wales so the taxi drivers were packed off to their respective training establishments and the potential Seamen/radar operators organised their kit, collected packed lunches from the galley and those chosen for *HMS Glendower* entrained for North Wales.

HMS Glendower

All that was known about *HMS Glendower* was that it was in the wilds of Wales near Pwllheli, an area I knew quite well from pre-war holidays in the area and had probably cycled past the site that became the camp.

The rail journey from RA to Glendower was a lengthy business on the overloaded wartime railways and took most of one day, all the night and a bit of the next day but on October 24th.1944 we clanked to a Halt in the middle of what appeared to be another holiday camp but identification was not possible due to the erasure of the name boards in accordance with wartime requirements but later discovered to be Pen y Chain Halt.

This, at last, was *HMS Glendower* and the history is interesting in that it was an embryonic holiday camp built by Billy Butlin at the request of the RN as an overflow to RA at a time when he was working for the Ministry of Defence.

The idea was that a coastal site must be found, well away from enemy activity, close to a railway with good communications and which could deal with the massive influx into the RN and could be built with a holiday camp in mind so that, after the war, it could easily be converted to such.

Billy found the ideal site at Pen y Chain Point and built what was to become the largest holiday camp in Europe, or,rather, that was the idea if the Allies won the war, what the plans were if the Axis had won is not recorded; one presumes it would have been a Kraft durch Freude centre and I would be typing this in German.

Thus, Nore Command General Orders for September 20th. 1940 state that *HMS Glendower* was to be used as a relief establishment to *Royal Arthur* and to be administrated by the Commander in Chief, Western Approaches Command.

From October 1st. 1940 her function to be:

A. Part 1. (Disciplinary) Training for H.O. (Hostilities Only) Seamen, S.B.As (Sick Berth Attendants), Cooks and Stewards. Part 2. Technical Training for H.O. eamen.

B. DEMS (Defensively Equipped Merchant Ships) Acting Seamen Gunners. Part 3. Training (HO Seamen who have completed Parts 1 & 2).

This then was the role *HMS Glendower* was to play in WW2, how many thousands were trained there I do not know but it must have been very many indeed by the time she was paid off and closed on September 1st. 1946.

The name *Glendower* was familiar to many as the famous Welsh patriot *Owain Glendwr*, suitably Anglicised for the RN and the ships crest being the Arms attributed to him described in the quaint and archaic language of heraldry: a demi lion erased, blue gorged with collar company white.

First action on arrival was a meal waiting for us then something straight from Kipling, each of us had to sign for and receive the King's Shilling, a splendid piece of tradition.

We were then formed into the standard Classes of fifty and allocated an Instructor, ours was Leading Seaman Withers, addressed as 'Chief'; poor devil, he worked and worried himself to a frazzle in an attempt to turn us into a smart class of Seamen, I hope we repaid his efforts in the end.

The Instructional Staff were, in the main, Petty Officers and Chiefs with a scattering of Warrant Officers; to us schoolboys they all looked ancient and probably were, most of them having been recalled from retirement.

Most of them were very hot on their technical subjects as well they might be after a lifetime in the RN but general educational talents, in a lot of cases, left a good deal to be desired.

One early observation to an elderly Petty Officer who did not know the difference between *magnetise* and *magnify* led him to ask me what my Father did as his had been a brickie, I ought to have known better.

The Ships Company must have been large, the Commanding Officer was Captain A.M. Williams RN with a staff of some eighty officers which included some dozen doctors, dentists and surgeons, fifteen Warrant Officers the remaining being instructional and administrators, a large proportion being RNVR.

Added to these were five Wrns officers and a large contingent of Wrns ratings who did all the usual jobs;there must have been well over one hundred of them and they lived in the camp surrounded by much barbed wire despite the tales of bromide in the tea.

The large number of Warrant Officers was notable, they were the Lower Deck equivalent of Admiral having sweated their way through the ranks and were experts at their craft, gunners, bosuns, wardmasters and so forth; probably most or all of them were drawn from reserve or retirement and unfit for sea duties but performed a valuable service in a training role where their expertise could be passed on. By now we were beginning to settle down and take stock of the situation and the relentless activity began to assume some definite order,there

HMS Glendower, parade ground

Morning Divisions (Wrns Parade)

really was a system in all the mayhem and we were all a part of it,very small cogs in a very large machine.

This system was overseen by King's Regulations and Admiralty Instructions and further expanded by the rules found in the Seaman's Manual wherein were enshrined all aspects of life for a Seaman and his trade and, tho' no-one ever saw this work due to the logistical problems of supplying the huge wartime intake, it was more than evident that the contents were indelibly engraved in the minds of our instructors and they passed it all on to us.

An example of the sinister influence exercised by this manual was that the supposed seven lateral creases in our bell bottom trousers were spaced in some direct ratio to the width and height of the book.

Nelson himself was not absent from all this, in fact one could be forgiven for thinking that he ran the RN, at least in part, and slogans attributed to him were emblazoned all round the mess hall, no doubt to spur us on to greater things.

The food at Glendower, and in the RN generally, seemed adequate and I never recall being hungry despite a very active life tho', from time to time, Joe and I would go down to the beach to gather winkles later to be boiled for us in the galley by Wrn Cook Bunty, the only personal contact I had with a Wrn whilst in the service, ratings being of an incredibly low order.

The training course was very hard work, not helped by being the middle of the winter and the North Wales coast at that time of the year is not noted for being particularly temperate.

All the course appeared to have been done at the double and I think Part 1 (Disciplinary) and Part 2 (Technical) were done together; it is difficult to be precise where one started and the other finished; apparently Part 1 was drill and weapons training, mostly on the parade ground where increasingly frustrated instructors trying to cram round pegs into square holes.

Part 2 (Technical) was more clearly defined and dealt with all aspects of Seamanship; bends and hitches, splicing, swinging the lead, anchors and cables, rigging, focsle work and sailing and rowing cutters and whalers in Pwllheli harbour, bleak in the extreme at that time of the year.

Added to the technical aspect was the gunnery and torpedo course,extending to several weeks in the gunnery school where considerable training was given on Armstrong Whitworth six-inch guns which, judging by the inscriptions, had been made for the Turks or similar and eventually found their way back here, probably as a consequence of WW1.

This weapon was standard in the RN at the time and endless drills were performed as we rotated round the gun crew;later we did a spell in the gunnery trainer in the dark and complete with thunderflashes and water flung in by bored Wrns.

Anyone caught skylarking or not paying attention was obliged to hold one of the six-inch projectiles for some considerable time and, as they weighed something in excess of a hundred pounds, it was not an exercise to be repeated.

After the six-inch gun was a stint on the four-inch QF and in this case we fired one such weapon from the battery at the end of the Point using a reduced charge and solid shot;the gun went off with a terrible crack and we expected to see the shell disappear over the horizon but it merely splashed into the sea not many yards off shore.

That night we were obliged to sleep in the ammo. hut close to the battery, or sleep if we could as it was horribly cold;no reason was given but no doubt it was all very symbolic and a foretaste of things to come. Next came the 20 mm Oerlikon cannon, this fearsome beast was largely for anti aircraft purposes with a range of some eight thousand feet firing armour piercing, explosive and tracer shells.

They all made a spectacular show as they arched into the sky from the Point, empty cases flying all around.

The course was completed after further instruction on the Point Five-Inch Browning machine gun and the mulitple (four) .303 machine guns, again, mainly for anti aircraft purposes.

Rowing at Pwllheli

Other weapons used by the RN were the Lee Enfield .303 rifle and the 9 mm Lanchester sub-machine gun, all of which we could strip blindfolded and frequently fired on the ranges.

Deflection shooting was practiced in a type of Dome Trainer wherein model aircraft came whizzing down a cable towards the gun position, with correct noises off; the gun was a sort of compressed air operated machine gun that fired small ball bearings illuminated by a bright light fixed to the gun and giving the impression of tracers.

There was also a model E-Boat operating in a similar manner, administrated by a couple of Wrns. who had little to do other than clear stoppages which were frequent.

In between all this activity were endless lectures and instructional films, some that spring to mind were Damage Control, First Aid and a rather gruesome one on VD and what happened if you got it..." If she's willing, she's got it and if she's got it you've had it" ran the slogan. Future radar operators were shown special, highly secret films dealing with radio and radar basics as a start for the course for RP3.

There were two sections to the radar operator branch, Gunnery and Warning, introduced by the Admiralty as a consequence of a reorganisation of the radar branch in 1944 and as I went to Warning some decision must have been made about this time tho' I have no recollection who made it.

Keeping Healthy was a essential part of being a Jolly Jack Tar and work in the gym was a major part of activities;the Physical Training Instructors (PTIs) being particularly hated as they always seemed dreadfully hale and hearty despite the cold wet weather and,to add to our misery,actually enjoyed being scantily dressed in T shirts (singlets then) and track suits.

A further extension of this PT was cross country running whereby we puffed our way around the roads near the camp; Afon Wen Laundry which we frequently passed is there to this day.

Captain taking the salute at morning divisions

Spare time was very restricted, there were only a couple of shore leaves during the course and, in any event, there was hardly anywhere to go other than Pwllheli or Porthmadoc and seaside towns in winter and wartime did not have much to offer other than a few pubs. and cinemas; there was another problem too as there had been scraps between Stroppy Jacks and RAF personnel from the nearby Penrhos airfield, famous for the pre-war 'Burning of the Bombing Range' saga so no doubt the RN considered it sensible to keep trainees in the Camp.

There was a Camp cinema showing all the current films, also a bar selling some watery beer, plus small canteens in the mess halls for the sale of nutty and odds and ends, should anything be available which wasn't often. Naturally most had to do guard duties around the Camp, one duty was guarding the Oerlikon, the sole defence against aerial attack and another,most unpopular job was to guard the beach at night in case of invasion.

We trudged up and down the shingle between Pen y Chain Point and Pwllheli suitably togged up for the awful weather and sporting a Lee Enfield Mk 1 with five rounds of much dented ammunition. Part of the farce was to meet our opposite number in the Coastguard and exchange the password which,of course, was Nelson.

What would have happened had we been confronted by the enemy is a matter for conjecture so perhaps it was fortunate that none appeared but it was useful experience and a warning as to what may be round the corner.

No training establishment would be complete without an assault course so naturally there was one at Glendower utilising several convenient topographical features where we slogged away.

Close by was a small farmhouse where some zealot managed to carry on farming surrounded by the frenzy of training and where we used to call for cheese sandwiches whilst on guard.

Halfway through the course there was a mild interlude thanks to Xmas but no shore leave; the RN managed a slap up Xmas dinner despite severe rationing for the civilians.

Towards the end of the course a mobile radar set arrived and was installed on a small hillock at the end of the Point, it was an Army set, possibly GL3 or similar consisting of a generator and small square rotatable cabin containing the equipment with an aerial array on the side and top so all the radar ratings trooped along to view this piece of technological wizardry and receive some brief instruction.

The crew were RN Combined Ops. personnel kitted out in Army battledress with RN insignia and caps; we were much impressed by this show of nonchalance in the middle of a super Pusser training establishment.

The course was now drawing to a close and in the last weeks classes who had completed their course went to Work Ship, *i.e*: help with the everyday maintenance, wearing No 3 dress, namely overalls, a considerable badge of distinction for us old salts among the newly arrived sprogs.

Thus days at Glendower were nearly ended, nearly because when the exams had been taken and passed and the class went on leave I managed to end up in Sick Bay with a high and unexplained temperature loosing a part of my leave in the process but whiling the time away cleaning vaccination needles; well, the war had to be won somehow.

Leave completed everyone returned to Glendower, collected kit and entrained for Fleetwood and thence to *HMS Valkyrie* in the Isle of Man for radar training.

HMS Valkrie Officer's Mess

HMS Valkrie

O f the journey from Glendower to Fleetwood no memory remains but it must have been overnight, most likely in a blackedout and unheated train for we arrived on the quayside in the early morning and, wandering the streets, were invited into a local mill for a cup of tea by some of the girls feeling a bit sorry for us.

In due course we boarded *SS Snaefell*, a twin funnel ship of the Isle of Man Steam Packet Company; she was a distinct oldie having been constructed by Fairfields at Govern in 1906 for G & J Burns for the Belfast run and called Viper; she was sold to the Isle of Man Steam Packet Company in 1920 for £160,000 and renamed Snaefell(4).

She displaced some 1730 tons and could carry 1700 passengers and had a crew of 61; used as a trooper in the early part of WW2 she was returned to the Isle of Man Steam Packet Company as one of the pair of ships maintaining the service to the Isle of Man.

Our trip on her was one of the last, for almost worn out, she was taken out of service for scrapping shortly after.

The ship was packed and the Irish Sea that day was very rough indeed and it took many hours to reach Douglas, a large proportion of the passengers being very seasick.

The place name Douglas derives from Gailk, the Celtic language of the Island and means Dark (or Black) Stream; the town is a classic Victorian holiday

SS. Snaefell (4) at Douglas.

resort with a wide sweeping promenade backed by imposing hotels and boarding houses, much in the manner of Llandudno and Colwyn Bay.

To the south of the town is the large rocky headland of Douglas Head, providing protection for the small, largely artificial, harbour which is ideally situated for access being a part of the town.

On March 3rd. 1945 Snaefell disgorged a pallid cargo onto the quayside, the different services sorted themselves out and went their various ways.

The expected Chief Petty Officer appeared from the crowd, very official in gaiters, three button jacket and three buttons on each cuff as appropriate to the rate but unfamiliar trade badges on his lapels; Telegraphists wings with a crown above and 'P' beneath, RPI we were to find, Radar Plot Instructor. Fallen-in in three ranks, rightdressed, left turned and quick march away from the harbour, past a fine Victorian clock and along Loch Promenade for a couple of hundred yards and halting outside a Naval establishment.

This was HMS Valkyrie and it was formed of the pre war hotels of Regent and Granville joined together with half of the wide roadway forming the promenade wired off to form a parade ground.

There was an elderly sentry and a ship's bell, this then was the barracks for the radar training school on Douglas Head, all well away from enemy action and, being on a island, security was reasonably assured.

There were actually two Valkyries, Valkyrie 1 was the radar training school, and Valkyrie 2 a co mural W/T training school for telegraphists. Once joining routine had been completed and messes allocated training commenced immediately; all classroom work took place in the barracks and all practical work on the sets in the school on Douglas Head.

There was a good deal of this classroom work mostly conducted by Warrant Officer Schoolmasters and was mainly concerned with electrical, radio and radar

Radar aerials at HMS Valkrie

Radar ratings at Douglas Head

theory, with much talk of strapped Magnetrons, waveguides, aerials, volts amps, watts and so on; radar was so secret at the time that all note-books were locked away after each lecture.

As previously mentioned, there were two sections to the radar branch, Gunnery and Warning, the former did their training in Douglas Head Hotel, a gloomy battlemented Victorian structure atop the Head and the latter (Air and Surface Search and Warning, (ASSW) was undertaken in a separate building purpose built by the RN; today it houses Manx Radio.

Valkyrie had been commissioned in July 1941 and styled The Royal Naval School of Radar Training; naturally there was a crest; a gold winged silver helmet and a motto '*Retia Beli Teximu*',We Weave the Nets of Battle, a sure give away to the Germans who were not averse to the same sort of thing themselves with Freya *et al*.

Ships of the RN were being fitted with radar, in some cases over a dozen to a battleship, faster than operators were being trained so there was a considerable backlog and this was met by Valkyrie operating 24 hours a day. Our class did set training some time in the middle of the night and we were obliged to form up outside the barracks and set off for the Head in total darkness with lamps at the head and tail of the column.

Douglas Head not only had the radar school but also spotting stations connected with *HMS Urley*, the Fleet Air Arm (FAA) airfield at Ronaldsway which carried out bombing and torpedo practices off the Head, in fact the whole of the Head was surrounded with barbed wire and access to the public totally denied, as well as most RN personnel, only those engaged on radar being allowed.

The first introduction to a radar set came soon after arrival and this proved to be a Type 281 air warning set with a range of over 100 miles; first impressions were that it appeared to be of bewildering complexity with a mass of coloured knobs, dials, meters, switches, co-axial cable, handles and cathode ray tubes.

It was the size of a bulky wardrobe and the transmitter, buried in the basement, the size of a small room; the instructor gave details of how the unit was switched on and a practical demonstration with the Cathode Ray Tube (CRT) lighting up with a vivid shimmering emerald green trace; on the left side a large blip caused by the ground returns and the top of the trace,an 'A' trace, looking like grass which was the term for it, this was the equivalent to noise in a radio set plus odd returns from waves and the like.

Turning a large wheel on the front of the set rotated the aerial so that it was pointing at the mountains of the Lake District some 60 miles away and, on the CRT appeared a large blip on the 60 mile range; our first echoes. Most of the instruction consisted of how to switch on the various sets, warm them up and get them fully operational, there was a ritual litany connected with all this but most of it now escapes me other than turning up the rheostat on the type 271 Magnetron to operating voltage, about 12,000v. This Magnetron had a large and powerful magnet that would magnetise most watches if you got too close, also the microwave radiation at 10 cms and about 70Kw was reputed to play havoc with ones reproductive processes and potential fathers were warned to stay well out of the way of the aerials. Detecting echoes was an acquired skill, transmissions and reception could be affected by the weather, the state of the set, the skill of the operators and so forth; many of the sets had wide beams and considerable

Type 281 radar receiver

winding backwards and forewards was required to obtain minimums each side of the beam and from that deduce maximum tho' the later 10 cm sets had a far narrower beam and did not have quite the same problems.

Weak echoes did not always appear above the trace but could be detected by a small depression on the underside.

Additional to the amplitude modulation of the A-trace was the intensity modulated PPI where the trace rotated as a radius of the screen and in sync. with the aerial thus showing a plan of the swept area with the ship in the centre, this had obvious advantages.

The A-trace was a five-inch tube with a green phosphor coating and the PPI a ten-inch tube with orange phosphor.

One gee whiz trick soon learned was to bridge a gap in the wave guide of the ten-centimetre sets with a finger nail and observe a large sizzling spark but saved from instant electrocution by the fact that it was Radio-Frequency (RF) energy.

38

My Radar History Sheet notes a pass with 75% on the 271 and 73% on the 281 tho' I do recall other sets such as 79,279,291 and 277 and a passing look at some of the gunnery sets, 274 and 275 spring to mind.

Due to the odd hours of training there was time available during the day and some of this was taken up rambling round the Island in so far as one could with trips on the fine Victorian tramway, which still ran as far as Ramsay, and visits to the local canteens and pubs.

I recall little of the sleeping and feeding arrangements but do recall the fog horn which seemed to blow most nights, a deep roaring bellow that shook everything.

There was a considerable staff at Valkyrie, the Commanding Officer was Captain Halfhide supported by some 40 officers, mostly instructors, seventeen of whom were WO Schoolies, plus half a dozen Wrn. officers and the usual large contingent of Wrns. ratings doing Cooks,Writers,Supply *et al.*

Also many Petty Officers and Chief Petty Officers as radar mechanics or instructors together with many old salts in ship's company as guards and the like.

In addition to RN trainees there were those of other nations as well, Dutch and French were noted but we tended to stick to our own classmates in this strange topsy turvy world.

Military presence on the Isle of Man was considerable and, apart from Valkyrie and Urley there was *HMS St.George*, previously Cunningham's Camp where Billy Butlin learned how to do it and now housing the Boys training establishment from *HMS Ganges* at Shotley plus the RN School of Music at Howstrakes Camp. The RAF was in occupation at Andreas and Jurby and the Island abounded with internees of all descriptions, from British Fascists to Non Fascist Italian West End Chefs, all scooped up together; next door to Valkyrie was a large hotel full of Air Training Corps and uniforms of all types abounded.

Valkyrie closed in 1946 having trained some 26,000 radar operators and mechanics for the fleet, how many were Gunnery and how many Warning is difficult to say but perhaps a ratio of 3 Gunnery to 2 Warning.

HMS Valkrie, radar school, Douglas Head

According to contemporary press reports after the war the equipment at Valkyrie was valued at £3M in 1945, possibly £200M today so a lot of taxes. During our course there were 1,000 under training and in 1942/3 some 1,100 so no wonder the place worked round the clock and was as busy as a beehive. The course finished at the end of March 1945; in the way of things some must have failed and supposedly reverted to Seamen and went their separate ways tho' we never heard.

It was time to say goodbye to the Isle of Man so kits were packed and steps retraced via *SS Snaefell* to Fleetwood and onwards to *HMS Collingwood* at Fareham for the plotting part of the course for RP3 qualification.

S.—1245C. (Established May, 1944.)   Page 1.

RADAR PLOT HISTORY SHEET.

To be attached to the rating's Service Certificate until final discharge from the Service, when this History Sheet is to be given to the man, together with his Service Certificate.

Name. LINDOP John B. Official No. JX56085 Port Division Devonport,
(Surname in BLOCK LETTERS.)

RECORD OF ACTION STATIONS IN SHIPS AT SEA.

To be filled in, in H.M. Ships at sea, when duties are performed **for not less than six months.**

Where a rating is found unsuited for any particular Radar Plotting duty, a notation to that effect is to be made in RED. Should any man be subject to severe seasickness, and therefore unsuitable for employment in ships smaller than cruisers, this fact is to be reported to the Commodore of the man's Depot, and a notation made on Page 1. If trained as spare number, note the duty in columns 5 and 6, and insert the word " spare " in column 7.

1	2	3	4	5	6	7	8
		RATING.					Initials of
Date	SHIP	Seaman	R.P.	Action Station	Duty	Ability	N. and F.D. Officers
			Date joined Royal Navy		22 Feb 44		

RECOMMENDATIONS FOR R.P. RATING AND SPECIAL QUALIFICATIONS NOT PROVIDED FOR ON PAGE 2.

To be filled in as soon as a man is recommended. Recommendations for qualified men are to be forwarded subsequently on Form S.1308 in accordance with the instructions on that form. Column 1 is to show the same date of recommendation as that on Form S.1308. Column 4 is to state the rating for which recommended, using the suffix (N.Q.) to distinguish a man not yet qualified by rating or experience and suffix (H) for a man highly recommended, whether qualified or not.

Date	SHIP	Present R.P. Rating	Recommendation or Special Qualification.	Initials of N. and F.D. Officers

HMS Collingwood

T he *HMS Collingwood* to which we were drafted from *HMS Valkyrie* on March 31st 1945 was the fourth to be so named and there were some illustrious ancestors. All were named after Admiral Cuthbert Collingwood who was second in command to Nelson at Trafalgar and took command on Nelson's death.

The first ship to bear his name was the last of the Wooden Walls, a battleship of some 2,485 tons with eighty guns launched in 1841 and scrapped in 1867.

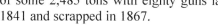

The second was an iron warship, a cruiser by WW2 definitions and weighing in at 9,500 tons; she served from 1887 until 1909 and the final ship was a Dreadnought type of 19,500 tons in service from 1910 to 1922.

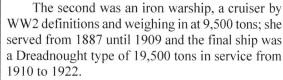

Our Collingwood was a stone frigate, as the RN called its shore bases, it was commissioned on Jan 10th 1940 and expressly built as a New Entry Training Establishment for Hostilities Only (H.O) ratings of the Seaman branch; it was a large establishment reflecting the urgency for crewing the ships of the rapidly expanding RN under pressure of war and intake was 1,000 every three weeks for a ten week course so activities must have been pretty frenzied.

Commanding Officer was Captain Bevan with a staff of 277 officers though a part of the activity at the base was an RDF school founded in 1942 and commanded by Captain G.M.K.Kebel-White with some half of the officer complement as instructors.

Collingwood was on the outskirts of Fareham, a part of the large RN presence in the Portsmouth area but accommodation was basic in the extreme being sectional wooden huts and a few buildings of a more substantial nature, due, we were told, to the fact that the establishment was built on marsh land tho' this did not stop the RN holding vast parades, the Admiralty was not to be denied ceremonials and rituals.

The only furniture available in the otherwise bare huts were iron bed-frames to accommodate the bedding carried about as hammocks, not even lockers for kit or any form of heating so we lived out of kitbags, the usual state of affairs in the RN.

Training started as soon as Joining Routine was completed and consisted of a three week course on how to utilise the information received from the radar sets, this taking the form of Plotting, both air and surface, R/T procedure and logging, Fighter Direction techniques and work in the Air Direction Room (ADR) where radar information was processed aboard the ships of the RN.

Again there was little shore leave tho' on one occasion Joe Lewis and I were obliged to visit RNB Portsmouth for reasons now unclear and noted the Holiest Object in the RN, namely HMS Victory.

On April 20th (Hitler's birthday incidentally tho' he was probably unaware of my involvement) we entrained for Rosyth on the battered wartime railways where *HMS Isle of Sark* awaited us, it was a long way and it must have taken ages but I cannot now recall a single detail of the trip.

JBL, Joe Lewis, Taylor, Red Rae

HMS Isle of Sark

In earlier, more Heroic Times, RDF (Radio Direction Finding) operators, as they were then called, were the beneficiaries of the sketchiest of training with a few minimal weeks at a basic training establishment to learn the rudiments of RN life, how to salute, a bit of drill, a short course at an RDF training school then straight to sea so as to crew, as quickly as possible, the rapidly expanding RDF service aboard ships of the fleet; these operators were specialists in the manner of Telecommunications and the like and worked a similar Watch structure.

In early February 1944 the Admiralty decided to reorganise the RDF branch, at the same changing the British terminology of RDF to that of the US Radar, and making it a subordinate part of the Seaman branch which would now be the prime qualification with radar as a non substantive addition; all RDF/radar ratings, from the commencement of the introduction of the equipment being Hostilities Only (HOs) personnel.

Additionally radar operators were split into Gunnery (Radar Control, RC) and Warning (Radar Plot, RP)with the various grades indicated by the usual stars and crowns, RPI, RP1, RP2, RP3 etc.

All this made for considerably longer courses and many skills were then available to us; it must have cost the hard pressed taxpayers a lot of extra money and seemed a waste of time and resources as we could all have been at the sharp end far quicker as the Seaman and Gunnery skills were hardly ever used, if at all, tho' no doubt someone at Admiralty had carefully worked it all out, or so we liked to believe.

One result of this reorganisation was a short sea course for aspiring radar operators (Warning) and who could quarrel with that decision; it was carried out aboard HMS Isle of Sark, one of a group of ships called the Radar Training Flotilla (RTF), the others being HMS Pollux an ex Russian ice breaker and HMS Caduceus, ex SS Manxman from the Isle of Man run.

Whether Pollux and Caduceus were operational as such at this time I do not know but Isle of Sark was and, as the name implies, she was ex SS Isle of Sark from the Southern Railways Channel Islands service in happier times. Built by Denny Bros of Dumbarton in 1932 she weighed some 2,110 tons but by the time the RN had finished she must have been a good deal more with all the armaments, radar and radio, extra accommodation, survival gear and so on.

In earlier times she, together with Pollux and Caduceus had picked up trainees direct from Valkyrie by docking in Douglas Harbour, thence carrying out training in the Irish Sea but, due to the increased mobility and threat of U-Boats now equipped with Schnorkels, it was considered prudent to transfer the operation to the Firth of Forth where we were drafted on April 21st.

The ship was boarded at Rosyth and put to sea immediately, passing under the famous Forth Bridge and into the wide estuary of the river.

After a meal and general settling into the routine of the ship it was time for bed, hammocks were pressed into use for the first time and some very interesting sights were observed as the less acrobatically inclined attempted to struggle into them.

Our mess was once a saloon with wide double stairs to the upper decks and accommodated many trainees.

The hammocks were just as well as the ship rolled violently but, tightly packed like sardines in a can but swaying gently from side to side,the first taste of real sea time had arrived.

Isle of Sark had recently returned from a refit, part of which was having a new bow fitted for, whilst on the way for the refit, she had been in collision with another ship, despite being loaded down with radar.

The major change was the installation of a type 277 radar atop a lattice mast between the foreward funnel and the bridge.

Otherwise she had two type 271 sets one either side of the bridge and type 291s on the mastheads, and, rather oddly, an indicator unit from a type 279 but fed by a type 291, or so it seemed.

The ship's company, it was said, was the original one from civvy days and inducted into the RN, presumably as T124s who received Merchant Navy pay, tho' this was never confirmed.

The Captain of Isle of Sark was Commander G.L. Bodoano and his First Lieutenant Lt/Cdr. C.E.Turner RNVR supported by some 14 other officers and, no doubt, a similar number of Petty Officers as instructors and radar mechanics. Attached to the RTF were three support vessels; two drifters, Yorkshire Lass, (Skipper S.Beckett RNR), and Jessie Tait; also an elderly submarine HMSm Otway which popped up in varying degrees and at inopportune moments so that we could be instructed in the tasks of detecting periscopes and hull down submarines, no easy task.

Drifter similar to Jessie Tate

HMS Isle of Sark

Lt. Cdr. C.E. Turner, RNVR,
1st Lieut. Of HMS Isle of Sark

HMS Otway

April 1945.
O/S Lindop standing to attention front rank, centre Morning Divisions, HMS Isle of Sark; the 1st Lieutenant, Lt. Cdr C. E. Turner RNVR on his final day aboard about to report to the Captain.

A periscope could be detected with the type 271 at some 1,500 yards and a surfaced submarine at about three miles with the type 271 and 291.

There was a lot of talk about RDF/radar/radiolocation being a British invention but, of course, this was a myth as Hertz himself had commented on the ability of wireless waves to be reflected by metal objects and one of the first reported successful radars was built by Christian Hulsmeyer, a German, in 1904, he called it the Telemobiloscope tho' it never got beyond being a scientific curiosity.

The radars of our day were being developed in many countries more or less at the same time tho' each was unaware of the others work.

Certainly the German Navy, the Kriegsmarine, was among the first users being fitted to many of the large units of their surface fleet *circa* 1935 but they never developed it to the extent the Allies did for varied reasons.

On Isle of Sark training continued and we struggled with the problems of hand rotated aerials as the ship rolled all over the place, at the same time rotating the aerial from one null to another, adding the two together and dividing by two for maximum echo then rotating to that bearing.

How many U-Boats were lost by that procedure was not revealed.

Later sets had power operated aerials so reducing the burden somewhat and the 10-centimetre sets had a beam narrow in plan so making it far easier to get a rapid and accurate bearing.

Height finding was a bit of a problem until the type 277 was fully operational though the situation was partly resolved by utilising the lobes of the types 279 and 281 for, as an aircraft flew through these lobes, the signal waxed and waned and when applied to a polar diagram the height could reasonably be deduced.

After a week of plodding up and down the Firth of Forth we came alongside at Rosyth and had a couple of days leave; Red Rae, Herbie Wiggins, Taylor and myself went off to Glasgow to see the sights and, it seems, Wiggins saw more than he bargained for but the rest of us went to the cinema and had rather a dull time tho' it was a relief to get away from the rigid and severe RN wartime discipline.

HMS Isle of Sark after refit with type 277 radar on tower

Back to Isle of Sark and another week of relentless plodding up and down the Forth; someone must have suggested that we went further out to sea because the Commanding Officer announced on the Tannoy that this would not be possible as there were reports of a U-Boat operating in the area and this was the closest I came to that deadly weapon.

The course was completed on May 7th and with strong rumours circulating concerning the probable collapse of the German forces, we entrained for the long journey to RNB Devonport, otherwise known as HMS Drake.

The actual results of all this radar training were not known until demobilisation when the Radar Plot History Sheet was among all the papers handed over, all that was known at the time was either pass or fail.

After the war Isle of Sark returned to her old job on the Channel Islands run tho', of course, stripped of all the RN equipment, and being pretty well worn out, was scrapped not long afterwards.

H.M.S.

Wartime Cap Tally.

First type RP3 trade badge. Gold for No.1; Blue for Tropical; Red for No.2.

RN 'Y' Scheme.   RDF Operator.

Later type RP3 trade badge.

Air Training Corps.   South East Asia Command   Wrekin College OTC.

HMS Drake (Royal Naval Barracks)

From earliest times during training the Royal Naval Barracks (RNB) were spoken of in hushed tones and with furtive looks over the shoulder, places awash with Brass Hats, Crushers, King's Regulations and Admiralty Instructions everything at the double or worse and Ultra Pusser (Pusser is a slang term for referring to the overall RN system and derives from Purser).

We were filled with foreboding, surely there could not be anything worse than the training establishments.

First introduction to this state of affairs was after completion of training on Isle of Sark when the various personnel on the course were despatched to their respective Port Divisions, in my case RNB Devonport. Filled with apprehension we stood to attention outside the Watch Office with its tall tower just inside the Main Gate of the barracks, our kit littered around; from the dark recesses of the doorway emerged a Petty Officer, Regulating; gaiters, white belt, long Watch Coat to his ankles, chain around his neck and a clip board with all our details clasped in his iron hand, a terrifying sight indeed.

He looked us up and down and observed, in Stentorian Tones, that 'you are now entering RNB, you will obey all senior rates, all officers will be saluted, all commands will be carried out at the double, you will be properly dressed at all times' and so on.

This was as bad, if not worse than had been predicted, life at RNB was going to be tough, we had arrived for better or worse.

RNB was a part of the manner in which the RN was organised.

From earliest times it was necessary to house crews from paid off ships in between voyages and the obvious place so to do would be the ports where the ships were based.

In the main these traditional ports were Devonport, Portsmouth and Chatham, respectively Guzz, Pompey and Chats.; Guzz derived the nickname from a said partiality of the denizens of the barracks for 'tiddley oggies', *i.e*: Cornish Pasties, and those who partook of this delight were said to be Guzzlers, hence the derivation of the name.

Most of the RN was housed in these Ports, also the ships of the Fleet were distributed according to the Port Divisions, many of them having been originally built there; it was all arranged according to a definite formula both for ships and, to a certain extent, the geographical origins of the personnel.

The Fleet Air Arm had its own Port Division at Yeovilton and the small ships, *i.e*: trawlers, drifters minesweepers and so on at Lowestoft.

Devonport thereby was home to a good 25% of the RN

First impressions of Guzz were indeed forbidding, the buildings dating from the 1890s were grey granite and looked for all the world like the ones comprising Dartmoor Prison, indeed, conditions in the prison were no doubt a lot better than those at Guzz.

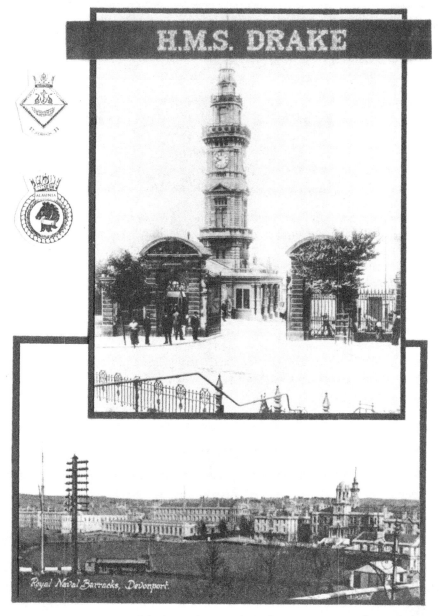

How many personnel the barracks were built for was a matter of speculation but the RN of pre war times consisted of about 100,000 men, expanded to some 880,000 in WW2 so Guzz had a lot more personnel than could reasonably be accommodated and conditions were cramped and Spartan in the extreme; the messdecks were vast empty rooms, barren in the daytime with the messdeck dodgers hiding behind the carefully arranged lockers, the spaces so enclosed doubling as the dining area.

One thing for which Guzz was famous was green pea soup; how this strange qualification arose no-one was too sure, neither did this culinary benefit extend to the other RNBs so far as I could tell tho' the quality and quantity of food available there and in the RN in general was quite good bearing in mind the rationing, shortages, mass catering

HMS Alaunia

problems *etc.* and certainly a lot better than currently available to the civilian population. At night the messdecks were a sea of hammocks, if, indeed, you were fortune enough to find a space to sling it and it was not uncommon to come off Watch or return from shore leave to find your hammock missing so a long search was required among the tightly packed snoring mass, locate the missing item,turf out the occupant and climb aboard.

Up to 1934 HMS Drake had been HMS Vivid but the name changed to accommodate the local hero, Sir Francis Drake of Armada fame.

Drake was the name of the whole RN presence in the Devonport area, of which RNB was a part; this encompassed a large part of the towns of Devonport and Plymouth covering the dockyards, hospital, gunnery school, Drake 2 and 4, anti gas school, ranges and all the other numerous RN activities.

All this was commanded by Admiral Sir Ralph Leatham KCB with a formidable staff of some eight hundred and fifty officers and an unknown number of ratings; RNB itself was commanded by Commodore 2nd. class (Captain jacked up for the appointment on a temporary basis) R.L.B. Cunliffe CBE and staff. I was a guest at RNB on three occasions,the first after completion of training from May 8th. to July 14th.

May 8th. was VE Day and I well recall the event being usefully employed dozing in my hammock when the announcement was made over the Tannoy to that effect; it was appropriate that Sir Harry Lauder had been singing 'Keep Right on to The End of The Road'.

On receipt of that information it was inevitable that there would be problems and problems there were tho' I managed to miss it all for some forgotten reason.

Almost to a man the whole rating complement of the barracks made for the Main Gate with the intention of painting the town very red indeed.

A brave and hopeless attempt was made by the Duty Crushers to halt this exodus and, when this failed to placate the mob, the Commodore himself was asked to intervene, agiitter in gold braid, but he too was swept aside and the town was painted extremely red indeed, the whole show ending up on Plymouth Hoe where the worlds biggest bonfire was lit.

It certainly was a day and night to remember tho' what happened as a consequence is not recorded for, by then, I had moved on to the nearby St.Budeaux Camp, a part of HMS Impregnable and then to HMFDT-13.

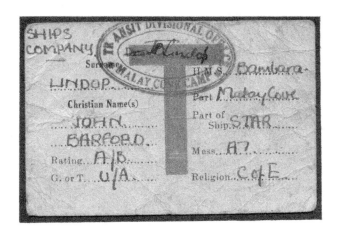

S. 247a (Established June, 1933, Revised Aug., 1934) H.M.S. BAMBARA

SURNAME PART DIV.OFFICE.
LINDOP. PART OF HQ.S.
CHRISTIAN NAME(S) SHIP A.D.R.
JOHN
BARFORD MESS HQS.
RATING A/B.
G. or T. G. RELIGION C of E.

(725) Wt. 21413/D7825 230m 7/44 S.E.R. Ltd. Gp. 671.

S. 247a (Established June, 1933, Revised Aug., 1934) H.M.S. Bambara

SURNAME PART 1st STAR
LINDOP. PART OF FLYING
CHRISTIAN NAME(S) SHIP CONTROL ADR.
JOHN
BARFORD MESS 5.
RATING A/B.
G. or T. G RELIGION C/E.

(997) Wt. 51778/D8110 200M 10/45 S.E.R. Ltd. Gp. 671

The next call to RNB was after leaving HMFDT-13, being drafted direct to Vicarage Road Camp, of which more anon tho' this closed shortly afterwards and we returned to RNB;it would have been October 25th to December 31st 1945.

There were the usual problems of what to do and the inevitable Working Parties to keep us out of trouble, one of which took us to the dockyards for work aboard HMS Alaunia (pictured right) converting from an AMC to a Heavy Repair Ship and we supplied some muscle heaving things around.

On one occasion leaving the ship I was offered a lift down by a crane operator so put my foot into the hook and grasping the chain with a sweaty hand, was whisked to one hundred and fifty feet in total terror then deposited on the dock floor; definitely not to be repeated.

Time was dragging and nothing seemed to be happening and I did not relish the next X years hanging around RNB so I went to the Drafting Office in a dungeon under our barrack block and knocked on the small window that put the occupants in touch with the real world, such as it was in RNB.

A Petty Officer Draftie opened the window, 'I'm fed up hanging around, can you fix me up with a draft, anything will do to get me out of RNB', I observed.

He retired to the depths to return with the observation that they had been looking for me for ages and where had I been ?

This was a standard ploy when they had lost track of anyone due to their administrative bungling and I was able to utilise the same stratagem when in a similar position in Malay Cove Camp.

They would look into the matter and let me know in due course; due course was next day when the Tannoy announced that A/B Lindop was to report to the Drafting Office where I learned that a radar operator was required for HMS Bambara at Trincomalee in Ceylon, the draft leaves the drill sheds tonight, get your gear together and be on it; it was Christmas 1945.

The cruiser, HMS Newcastle was in the dockyard and would be setting sail shortly, my draft had arrived and although I did not know it at the time, it would be two years before I saw RNB again.

The third and final visit to RNB was on return from Ceylon on December 24th 1947 so Xmas in the barracks once again.

There was the usual bellowing at the Main Gate but this time we were seasoned salts and, anyway, we would all be 'outside' in a few weeks time so who cared about Regulating Petty Officers.

Joining Routine was carried out with the usual visits to the Divisional Office, Regulating Office, Sick Bay, Pay Office, Mess and so forth so that we were, once again, inducted into The System.

What would have happened had all this been disregarded is difficult to say, but there were rumours that RNB was full of Faceless Men who pursued their way around looking important and carrying some official piece of paper but actually doing nothing as no-one was aware of their presence; I suppose some of them are probably there to this day.

After Joining Routine there was fourteen days leave to come then Demob to look foreward to as it was now March 1948, my Demob. Number was 63 and it was looming large on the horizon but, before that, back to the war which still had to be won.

HMS Impregnable (St. Budeaux Camp)

This Camp was located between HMS Impregnable and the shore of Weston Mill Lake opposite RNB and the dockyards and officially an extension to HMS Impregnable; it was a site that sloped steeply towards the Lake and afforded an excellent view of all the dockyard complex and the ships therein, which included a monitor HMS Roberts and a replica of the Golden Hind.

Accommodation was a group of some twenty Nissen huts together with a brick built HQ building, the huts were bare in the extreme in much the same manner as those at Collingwood, with no furniture at all other than bed frames for our hammocks and kit was stored in kit bags as usual; neither was there any sign of heating arrangements which wasn't too bad during May until July 14th when we left but the thoughts of winter there were daunting.

There was little to do other than hang around and join the usual working parties, the high points of the day being Postie and meal times, plus the odd run ashore for a minor binge as funds might allow.

An interesting eccentricity at the Camp was that the Bosun's Mate, instead of the usual Call, indulged himself with a hand operated bellows fog horn, splendid in its brass, leather and wood and he hooted himself variously around the Camp dispensing whatever gen their Lordships required.

Food was adequate but on one quite memorable occasion things went slightly haywire in a rather peculiar manner; in this instance we were all sat in the mess waiting for the servers to bring breakfast, as a rare treat, scrambled eggs on toast, a considerable delicacy.

Eggs were not the familiar things of today with shells and so forth but a powder formed by dehydrating the stirred up eggs,this was 'reconstituted' by adding water and cooking but in this instance, and unknown to the cooks, the powder was contaminated by countless ants eggs, laid in mysterious circumstances in places unknown.

The meal had been prepared the previous day and placed in heaters for the morning; when warmed up all the eggs hatched creating highly mobile scrambled eggs much to the consternation of the assembled multitudes who crowded round to observe this strange trick of the cooks.

What we did get for breakfast I no longer recall and the strange presence of the ant eggs was never explained.

One of the hazards of war !

Round about this time a notice appeared in HQ asking for RP3s to volunteer for submarines as radar was now being fitted to all of them and outstripping the supply of trained operators; all sub. crews were volunteers, got extra pay and wore appealing white jerseys; discipline, it was said, was easier in the small communities and anyway it would get me out of loafing around St.Budeaux so I put my name on the list, sat back and waited.

When the draft arrived it was not to subs. much to my disappointment, but to something called HMFDT-13 and as the whole of the class except Joe Lewis was going it must have a very strong radar activity.

Poor old Joe thought this was a form of discrimination but it only turned out to be the hand of fate, somewhat unfairly applied.

He lived in Bishops Castle and I attempted to visit him forty three years later to find that he had died of a heart attack only weeks before, it upset me greatly as we had gone all thro' training together and I had always cherished the rather romantic notion that while Joe was there, even if we did not meet, in some mysterious way he was my link with the old RN.

Now he is gone my RN has gone too, a fact very much confirmed when starting the research for this history.

HMFDT-13

The prerequisite of any invasion is complete mastery of the air, no mastery of the air, no invasion. Operating a large air striking force in this manner requires control close to the point of operations, relatively easy when on land but more difficult when the invasion is a sea bourne one, as in the case of Operation Neptune, the naval part of Overlord for D-Day.

In this latter case a floating operations room was required and though it is correct that large surface units such as battleships were well equipped for such activities they were too vulnerable pottering along close to a heavily defended enemy coast so an alternative solution had to be sought. This was resolved by building a special class of ships as floating operations rooms especially for this type of invasion, carrying out the exercise from sea until the RAF could take over with land based radars so for this purpose three classes of ships were prepared.

The first, called LSFs (Landing Ships Fighter Direction) were Antwerp, Ulster Queen, Palomares and Stuart Prince, all conversions from merchantmen of about three to five thousand tons.

The second types were FDTs (Fighter Direction Tenders), comprehensive conversions of British built LSTs(1) (Landing Ship Tank) and were Boxer, Bruiser and Thruster of riveted construction and with steam engines, tho' ultimately only Boxer was so converted; the third types were also ex LSTs, in this case American LST(2)s, FDT-13, 216 and 217, of all welded construction with Diesel engines.

Although I was not to become ship's company aboard FDT-13 until July 1945 for the second commission to take part in the invasion of Japan it is worth recording her history and that of her sisters, 216 and 217 as an example of a highly specialised weapon that is very unlikely to appear again.

The early history of FDT-13 started in the shipyards of the Dravo Corporation in Pittsburg, U.S.A. when her first plates were laid down on September 1st. 1942. She was launched on January 5th. 1943 by Mrs. Jean Brackman and transferred to the RN on April 3rd. 1943; so far as can be discovered she had no operational life with the US Navy.

As built she displaced some 1,625 tons, was 328 feet long by 50 wide and with a draught of between 3 and 9.5 feet depending on loading.

Power was supplied by two Diesel engines with an output of 1,800 HP and producing a flat out, 'flank' speed of 11 kts. but cruised at substantially less hence the US Navy nickname for LST as Large Slow Target.

Original armament was intended to be one 12 pdr. and six 20 mm Oerlikons and the crew being 86, standard for LSTs.

FDT 216 and 217 were identical but built by the Chicago Bridge & Iron Company and transferred to the RN during September 1943.

His Majesty's Fighter Direction Tender "13" in London Graving Dock. December 1945.

LST 13 arrived at Liverpool June 13th. 1943 and went immediately to the Clyde for repairs, docking there on June 14th. with repairs taking until Aug. 23rd; on October 8th. she was at Greenock, again for repairs until November 9th. Next she appears at Southampton on December 3rd where she remained until December 20th; on December 24th. she was under passage to the Clyde again, arriving on December 31st. so it was Christmas at sea for the crew.

This time the purpose was for conversion to a Fighter Direction Ship, scheduled completion mid-February 1944.

216 and 217 followed similar paths and arrived at Messers John Brown shipyard on the Clyde at the same time as FDT-13 so it is evident that the conversion plans were common to all three and were to be known by the Code word 'Baccy'.

On Feb.14th. they were referred to as 'tenders' for the first time with completion dates as February 19th. 1944 tho' later extended to March 1st.

From March 10th. to April 7th. they were all at Glasgow, no doubt for more specialised work and where the conversions were completed.

Actual work on the hull only required welding up the bow doors plus the installation of large masts to carry all the communications aerials.

The interior volume, latterly the tank deck,was converted into the various offices required for the operations rooms, consisting of a Filter Room, Communications Office, Cypher Office, Air Control Room, Radar Receiving Room, as well as a D/F Office for RN DF equipment and aft was the Transmitter Room, Transceiver Room, Aircraft D/F (RAF VHF equipment), Radio Countermeasures Office (RCMs) and W/T storeroom.

To power all this extra load were four additional Diesel generators.

For the first commission the radars fitted were an RAF Type 8F 200 m/c GCI on the bows with a range of about 60 miles together with a height finding capability and an RAF Type 11 50 cm. set for use against low flying aircraft fitted amidships all with Mk 3 IFF and an AI radar beacon aft.

Three major and five minor masts carried all the radio aerials, beacons and HF/DF;fitted were 8 VHF and 9 HF R/T and W/T, a VHF/DF Type FV4 and 'Y' Type FV3; the crew, including the RAF detachment, estimated at about 250.

More defensive Oerlikons were installed but much reduced in their fields of fire by the mass of rigging, aerials, masts and general obstructions.

Ballast consisted of a layer of pig iron on the upper deck and over the operations room, rather vaguely secured by heavy wire mesh and doubling as a rudimentary armour plate; it was all regarded with grave misgivings.

On April 21st all three left Methil on the Forth and on April 24th. they were in the Humber until May 14th, more than probably at Immingham having the pig iron fitted, and from there to Southend arriving May 15th. tho' 217 detoured to Cardiff for repairs.

By May 26th. all were in the Portsmouth area getting ready for Operation Neptune, the naval part of Operation Overlord.

D-Day was June 6th. and all FDTs were part of Force J controlled by HQ ship Hiliary,an LSH(L).

FDT-13 was commanded by Ltt. Cdr. R.A. Crozier R.N.R. and a staff of six officers including a Surgeon Lieutenant.; 216 was commanded by Lt. Cdr. G.D. Kelly and four officers and 217s Commanding Officer was Lt. Cdr. F.A. Smythe also with four officers.

During the assault phase of D Day FDT-13 was positioned in the shipping lanes for early warning and control of fighter aircraft giving defensive cover to those lanes; the position was referred to as 'Piccadilly Circus'.

FDT 217 was positioned seaward of the British beaches and was the 'master' FDT. Whilst FTD 216 dealt with the American beaches and controlled all British and American fighter aircraft operating in the area.

HMFDT 13

Between June 6th. and June 24th. a total of 76 enemy aircraft were destroyed as a consequence of the interceptions under FDT control.

All FDTs were overcrowded, had inadequate air conditioning, the operations rooms were too hot and there were a lack of escape routes on top of all the other problems thus FDT became nicknamed Floating Death Trap.

On the night of June 22nd. FTD-13 was unsuccessfully attacked by Ju 88 aircraft whilst on patrol and on June 9th. FDTs 216 and 13 had been withdrawn to the Portsmouth area.

On July 7th FDT 216 was attacked by a Ju 88 and sunk by torpedo with five of the RAF section being killed tho' the rest of the crew were rescued from the sea, a remarkably small number of casualties.

On July 17th. FDT-13 was at Plymouth and FDT 217 in the Clyde where it remained until June 22nd, 1945.

On July 30th. FDT-13 was on passage to the Mediterranean and much involved in operations in Italy, North Africa and the invasion of Southern France; it was at Bizerta on August 14th and then variously at Naples and Southern France for Operation Torch, Taranto, the invasion of Greece and back to the UK via Gibraltar to arrive at Sheerness on January 29th. 1945 and was still there on February 20th.

Some time in early January 1945 the Admiralty issued instructions that FDT 217 was to be taken in hand by Messers London Graving Dock at Poplar for refit and preparation for service in the Far East to take part in the proposed invasion of Japan, plans for which would have been well advanced at that stage; Admiralty also asked for a report on defects but these must have been excessive as a signal was sent that FDT-13 be diverted in lieu.

On February 13th. 1945 FDT-13 was reported as being in London for refit with various dates for completion tho' by July 2nd. she was 'ex trials' despite a major fire in one of the generators in March.

FDT-13 Refit Number was 'ER 9916' and quite a lot of work had been done on her, the most obvious change being that the RAF Type 11 had been replaced by an RN Type 277 on a lattice tower to give better range; additionally a Type 291 was fitted to a small mast in front of the bridge.

Armament was increased by the addition of a pair of 40mm. Bofors, one each side and the whalers replaced with LCPs.

Internally ventilation was improved and better crew quarters arranged.

All this time there was a nucleus crew aboard and the ship never decommissioned tho' there were social problems in that no power was available and the facilities of a destroyer Brissenden, which was tied up alongside, had to be utilised.

FDT-13 was just inside the Graving Dock and the draft, making up some 80% of the ship's company, went aboard on July 15th; there was an all pervading smell of diesel oil that remains with me to this day, still evoking memories of first going aboard FDT-13 forty three years ago.

Commanding officer was Lt. Cdr. F.J.Storey RNR and his First Lieutenant was Lt. S. Burnaby Davies RN (known as 'Laughing Death') with eight other

officers including Surgeon Lieutenant N. McSwan; a much larger officer complement than on the previous commission.

Rating complement must have been similar to the previous commission, some 240 or so which included an RAF section to operate and service the GCI, the RAF apparently being of the view that they could not leave their radars to the mercies of us rough sailors.

After a matter of a very few days to settle in and get the ship sorted out we were off and on July 29th. slipped out of the dock for Sheerness to pick up stores and ammunition, hard work indeed; next stop was Tilbury for de-gaussing then off to the Clyde where we tied up alongside Boxer and took on board very many drums of oil; Boxer was crewed by many of our classmates from training days, one name survives, Cockburn, I wonder were he is now?

Of the crew of FDT-13 few names can now be recalled; Burnaby Davies, the lst.Lieut. McKay an AA3 who looked after the ammo. stores, Liptrott, a Seaman who had married just before the commission and made some amazing claims, I hope it was all put right in the end Herbie Wiggins was there as was Red Rae; L/S Pope our mess Killick who was i/c EVT (Educational and Vocational Training) to prepare us for the hurly burly of civvy life; Wood from our mess who had his name emblazoned on the back of his overalls in large white letters, always a mistake in retreat. Bill Bradshaw too but the rest is now a blank.

FDT-13 sailed for Malta but, *en route*, stopped off at the Isle Of Man for trials with HMS Queen, an Escort carrier, so that the radars could be calibrated.

We had a run ashore in Douglas and were interested to have a look at Valkyrie, still churning out radar operators; it made us feel quite like old hands at the game.

The trials must have been satisfactory as FDT13 then set off for Malta, crossing the Bay of Biscay without incident and down the coast of Portugal; being August it was pretty hot and night watches were quite pleasant which made a change.

I no longer recall if we stopped off at Gibraltar but otherwise went through the Straits into the Mediterranean where it became very hot indeed so at nights I slung my hammock from some convenient spot and slept in the open watching the sparkling phosphorescence and listening to the slap and splash of FDT-13's progress towards an unknown fate.

Hammocks were the de rigeur for most lower deck ratings, they were warm and comfortable and, of course, saved a great deal of space which was the general idea for the Wooden Walls and had carried on into the modern navy.

This was just as well as many ships of the WW2 period were designed before much of the modern technology came into use in the form of Asdic, HF/DF, radars, of which there might be many sets to a ship, and all this had to be found space where none was originally designed.

When that lot was installed room then had to be found for the operating personnel and they were crammed in where possible, sometimes were it wasn't and it made for a situation where bunks would be unacceptable.

Apart from those plus features hammocks were heavy, awkward and cumbersome when added to the bulky and heavy kitbags and other kit; it must have added a great deal to RN transport costs never mind the problems for the ratings who had to cart it all about.

Every morning it was "Wakey, Wakey, Lash up and Stow" and woe betides the unfortunate who did not lash his hammock in accordance with the Seamans Manual, none of your Granny knots here, then correctly stow it in the nettings provided on every messdeck.

Even the fact that one had a hammock was no guarantee that space to sling it would be available with all the extra crew crammed in and frequently one had to sleep on the deck or the tops of lockers and so on.

In respect of space FDT-13 was unusually well served as the operations block did not fill the tank space by any means, leaving quite a large area behind the hull doors that was utilised as a cinema and also had quite a large complement of bunks so I transfered myself there away from the hammock space by the showers; hammocks were a lot more stable than bunks, slung fore and aft they eliminated most of the worst of the ships movements, particularly rolling; this was not the case with bunks which were provided with sides to keep the occupant in place and, on occasion, it was necessary to hang on quite firmly.

Among the social features FDT-13 had a piano, no doubt given by some wellwisher; from time to time it was hauled to the upper deck and sing songs were organised; I suppose it was kept in the Wardroom and the thoughts of heaving such an object around a warship with the small hatches, steep ladders and so on were formidable, nevertheless, it was done.

FDT-13 also had a trumpet player who doubled as a bugler tho' he had to be hidden in the wheelhouse for entering and leaving harbour in case the local Admiral spotted this heresy.

There was also a dhoby firm set up by a enterprising Irishman who nearly monopolised the small dhoby room; dhobeying was a problem as the water was salt and required the special RN salt water soap tho' hammocks could be trailed astern on the lashings, the salt water and turbulent wake doing quite a good job in getting them clean.

Half way to Malta FDT-13's engines started to play up, first one would 'fall over' then the other; on one occasion both packed up at once and we drifted about feeling a bit silly and thankful it was calm and that the U-Boat threat no longer existed; the problem was probably dirty fuel clogging up the injectors, or so the buzz went; it was an ill wind however, as these lapses were used for a bit of swimming tho' the idea of the nearest land being some distance under the keel did not appeal so I stopped aboard, as did many others.

Spouting whales looked like shell bursts to edgy crew, flying fish skimmed the wavetops and dolphins swept around the bows and on one occasion the sea suddenly became as smooth as a sheet of glass with a clear demarkation that stretched to the horizon tho' what the reason was we never discovered.

Naturally life on one of His Majesty's warships was not all lying in hammocks or watching the fish at the expense of the taxpayer, there were serious things afoot and progress towards Japan was marked by knocking the ship's company into shape to act as a team and in the case of the radar personnel that was both in the ops. rooms and in Seaman duties; as latter we did watchkeeping, lookouts,

Lt.S.Burnaby Davies, 1st Lieut. HMFDT

entering and leaving harbour and so on, as radar my main duty was on the MADP (Main Air Display Plot).

This duty consisted of standing on the reverse of a large transparent Perspex plotting board and inscribing on it information passed by the radar; ranges, bearings, numbers of aircraft etc. and on the other side sat a FDO (Fighter Direction Officer) who attempted to make some sort of sense of the material on the board and determine the likely direction and intention of the attacking force and vector defending fighters to deal with them. On top of that I was also on the Type 277 radar so we were kept very busy.

In rough weather the ship rolled in a quite alarming manner, not improved by all the top weight and we were convinced that the bows could be seen to move independently of the stern as FDT-13 corkscrewed along at 8 knots.

According to the Pink List FDT-13 arrived at Malta on August 22nd. to find a large 'VJ' painted on Fort St.Angelo; whatever the correct date of arrival it was clear that the war was over, in fact on August 15th. and had been brought about by some mysterious agency called an atom bomb, used on two of Japan's major cities by the Americans.

Newspapers were obtained as soon as possible and these were filled with speculation as to how this magic device worked; one thing was certain however, it had save us and thousands more from the horrors of a full invasion of Japan and a very likely trip to Davey Jones' Locker, FDT-13 being a very visible and highly vulnerable target for the Kamikaze brigade.

Most of us had seen ex-prisoners of the Japs. and were certainly well aware of the treatment dished out so there was not the slightest sympathy for their being atom bombed, nor has that view changed.

FDT-13 first anchored in Grand Harbour then moved up to St. Pauls Bay where we all went swimming in the tropical waters and had a bit of shore leave; Malta seemed dry, dusty and a bit barren also severely damaged by the recent bombing, in fact the wreck of a partly submerged tanker was still there just inside the entrance to Grand Harbour, a relic of the heroic Malta convoys. The stay at Malta was noted mainly for the fruitful, or fruitless, painting ship with liberal applications of grey paint.

Alas, this lifestyle did not last very long so, according to the Pink List, FDT-13 arrived back in the Clyde on September 14th. having stopped off at Gibraltar.

The Pink List, by the way, was one of a series of Red, Blue, Green and Pink Lists whereby the Admiralty could keep track of all its ships, different classes having different colours as appropriate, all a formidable but essential task and one could tell within days, sometimes hours, where any particular ship was located; there was also a companion list, the Navy List detailing all officers in the RN; Royal Navy, Royal Naval Volunteer Reserve, Royal Naval Reserve, Royal Canadian Navy, Royal Australian Navy, Royal New Zealand Navy, Royal Indian Navy, Women's Royal Naval Service (Wrns) plus all the other 'colonies', Ceylon, Zanzibar, Hong Kong etc.

All these were listed by ship as well thus it was possible to tell who was what and where at any time; unfortunately no such information existed for Ratings which is hardly surprising as there were in excess of seven hundred thousand of us in June 1945.

Back in the Clyde FDT-13 anchored and was nearly cast ashore after dragging her anchor in a ferocious storm so we were all hauled out of our hammocks in the middle of the night to sort things out; this was the last bit of drama as eighty one radar ratings left FDT-13 about October 1st for return to Royal Naval Barracks (RNB).

I can still see FDT-13, grey and lonely, wallowing in the swell of the the Clyde. FDT-13 proceeded to London on October 19th. with the remaining crew; she arrived on October 29th. and was in for repairs December 3rd. and trials on December 10th.

About this time a photo was taken by the lst.Lieut. showing her, rust streaked and a bit forlorn, in the Graving Dock at Poplar in exactly the same place we had started from; FDT-217 in the background.

On December 28th she was in Plymouth, yet another Christmas at sea, getting ready for the trip across the Atlantic; by February 27th. she was transferred back to the US Navy at Norfolk, Virginia and on June 5th. was struck

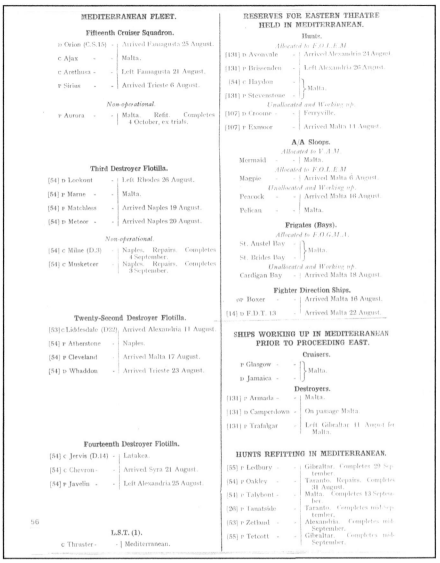

Extract from the "Pink List" 2nd July 1945

off the US Navy List. FDT-217 followed a similar route being returned to the USN April 1946.

FDT-13 was sold to Luria Bros. for scrapping on October 14th. 1947 and no doubt FDT-217 followed a similar fate.

FDT-13 had lasted some 1,870 days, I do not know what she originally cost thus interest on capital nor depreciation but daily running costs must have been considerable, all in all, not a very cost effective exercise but, of course, wars are not seen from the point of view of financial cost effectiveness.

Today none of these interesting ships remain except the rotting hulk of FDT-216, somewhere beneath the waves off Cape Barfleur and with five of the crew still aboard, a sad monument to the folly, wastefulness and stupidity of war.

ALL PREVIOUS COPIES OF THE "O.U." NAVY LIST
ARE TO BE DESTROYED.

TO BE KEPT LOCKED UP

O.U. 5513 (4)45

THE

NAVY LIST

CONTAINING

LIST OF SHIPS, ESTABLISHMENTS, AND OFFICERS OF THE FLEET

APRIL, 1945

VOLUME I

Alphabetical Indexes

AURIGA.

Lieutenant	R. Banner-Martin, DSC	26 Mar 46
	(In Command.)	
Lieutenant	E. L. M. Moss	6 Sept 46
	W. G. Edwards	3 Mar 46
	J. B. Rae	26 Apr 46
Tempy. Lieut. (E)	D. W. Laidlaw	6 Nov 44
Tempy. Sub-Lieut., R.N.V.R.	R. S. Mills	— May 45

Al ROCHS.

Lieutenant (E)	P. M. Mansell-Pleydell	25 June 45

AURORA. (Po.)

Commander	J. W. McClelland, DSO	24 Dec 45
	(In Command)	
Lieutenant	S. M. Beresford, DSC	— May 45
	P. Goode	— Oct 45
	F. A. Cobb	25 Apr 46
Commander(E), R.N.R.	W. D. Boosey, RD	22 May 46
Lieutenant (E)	W. G. Lockyer	— Feb 46
Tempy. Lieut. (E), R.N.V.R.	D. W. Barthelmas	8 Mar 44
Tempy. Surg. Lieut.-Com., R.N.V.R.	A. A. Robertson, MD, CHB (act)	— Feb 45
	H. C. Maingay, MB, CHB (act)	2 Apr 45
Tempy. Lieut. (S), R.N.V.R.	A. R. W. Reynolds	— Sept 45
Tempy. Sub-Lieut. (E)	A. J. Richardson	— May 45
Tempy. Sub-Lieut. (E), R.N.V.R.	H. L. Pratt	21 Apr 45
Sub-Lieut. (S)	C. H. H. Owen	4 Mar 45
Cd. Gunner	W. J. Overy (act)	28 Nov 44
	E. G. Wye	— June 46
Tempy. Wt. Shipwright	E. A. Baldwin	— Oct 45
	L. G. Firth	19 Jan 46
Wt. Engineer	E. D. Neville	— May 45

AUSONIA. (Ch.)

Captain	C. A. G. Hutchison, DSO, OBE (ret)	— Dec 45
	(In Command)	
Commander, R.N.R.	E. B. Clarke, RD	4 Oct 46
Lieut.-Com.	W. J. Collier	— Oct 45
Lieut.-Com. (E)	D. O. Bullen	— Apr 46
Lieutenant (E)	C. H. M. Townsend	11 Feb 46
Tempy. Lieut.(E)	R. J. Doble	20 July 43
	N. N. White	— May 46
Tempy. Chaplain, R.N.V.R.	Rev. E. C. W. Rusted	1 Dec 44
Commander(S)	A. W. Richards (act)	31 May 44
Tempy. Surg. Lieut., R.N.V.R.	K. H. Bassett, MRCS, LRCP	26 May 46
Tempy. Sub-Lieut., R.N.V.R	J. L. Roberts	— June 45
Tempy. Sub-Lieut.(E)	A. Lobley	— Feb 46
Tempy. Sub-Lieut. (S), R.N.V.R.	F. C. Knight	8 Feb 46
	J. R. Manning	5 Feb 46
	E. C. Tidder	15 Nov 45
Tempy. Cd. Gunner	(T) G. R. Rawlings (act)	1 Jan 43
Cd. Boatswain	F. V. Naylor (act)	— Apr 45
Cd. Engineer	J. G. Revolta	28 July 43
Tempy. Wt. Ord. Offr.	H. G. Hannan	— Jan 46

BADGER.

	(Parent Ship, Harwich.)	
Captain	G. N. Rawlings, DSO, DSC (act)	15 Jan 46
	(In Command and as N.O.I.C. Harwich)	
Secretary	Tempy. Lieut.-Com. (S) T. H. Messenger, RNVR (act)	— Sept 45
Commander, R.N.R.	R. E. Brett, DSO, DSC, RD (act)	12 Nov 45
Tempy. Lieut.-Com., R.N.R.	W. Brearley (act)	5 Nov 45
	H. C. F. Dawes (act)	12 Mar 46
Tempy. Lieut.-Com., R.N.V.R.	R. E. Willson (act)	— Oct 45
Tempy. Lieut.-Com., R.N.V.R.	A. S. Miller, DSC (act)	15 June 45
Lieutenant	J. A. Jago (act)	— Oct 43
	G. O. Harrell	30 Apr 46
Tempy. Lieut., R.N.V.R.	G. D. Smedley	— Oct 45
	F. J. Murphy	11 Mar 46
	L. A. Jennings	25 Feb 46
	R. T. Hirons	6 Apr 46
Lieut.-Com. (E).	J. B. Newton, MBE (act)	7 Oct 41
Tempy. Lieut.-Com. (E)	G. G. Wood (act)	20 Oct 45
Lieutenant (E)	A. W. Fairhead OBE	15 June 43
Tempy. Lieut. (E), R.N.V.R.	J. Milne	9 Nov 45
	H. Rennie	5 Dec 44
Surg. Com.	D. C. Drake, MRCS, LRCP	30 May 46
Commander (S)	H. S. Howell	22 Oct 45
Lieut.-Com. (S)	J. Storey (act)	15 Feb 46
Tempy. Surg. Lieut., R.N.V.R.	R. G. Davies, MB, BS	27 May 46
Tempy. Surg. Lieut. (D), R.N.V.R.	A. D. L. Paterson, LDS	17 Jan 46
	A. Ferrari, BDS	25 Mar 46
Lieutenant (S)	J. Crowley	1 Apr 46
Tempy. Lieut. (S), R.N.V.R.	E. J. Reynolds	13 Jan 44
	H. L. Kelly	25 Oct 43
	J. W. Gourlay	25 Mar 46
Tempy. Elect. Lieut., R.N.V.R.	W. Duffus	1 Dec 45
	D. E. French	31 Mar 46
Tempy. Sub-Lieut., R.N.V.R.	G. McInnes	12 June 45
	B. P. Roberts	25 Feb 46
	J. Harvey	25 Apr 46
	R. Lennie	6 May 46
	S. T. Drummond	13 May 46
Tempy. Sub-Lieut. (E), R.N.V.R.	J. J. Potter	21 June 45
Tempy. Sub-Lieut. (S), R.N.V.R.	A. S. Robertson	16 Jan 46
Tempy. Lieut. (Sp. Br.), R.N.V.R.	D. A. Cox	18 May 46
Tempy. Sub-Lieut. (Sp. Br.), R.N.V.R.	A. J. Aldridge	15 May 45
	J. E. Young	20 Oct 45
	A. J. Aldridge	26 Nov 45
Tempy. Cd. Gunner	J. King (act)	20 Dec 44
Cd. M.A.A.	G. J. N. Hebbourn	16 Oct 44
	(Naval Provost Marshal)	
Tempy. Cd. Shipwright	C. R. Smith, MBE (act)	14 Nov 44
Cd. Engineer	D. F. Westbrook	17 Aug 44
	T. W. Fyson	3 July 45
	P. W. Hoad (act)	8 Sept 45

Tempy. Sub-Lieut. (Sp. Br.), R.N.V.R.	{ I. F. Newman.............. 30 May 44 { W. H. Burrows.............. — June 44	
Tempy. Cd. Gunner	{ J. W. Elliott (act)............ 14 Nov 44 { (T) A. T. Warne, MBE (act) 24 May 44	
Schoolmaster (C.W.O.)	}J. R. Ellis, BSC (act)......... 12 Sept 42	
Tempy. Boatswain	}C.T. Denby (act)............. 28 Nov 44	
Tempy. Boatswain (A/S)	{ L. R. Field............. 28 June 42 { †J. J. Welch.............. — Mar 45 (For Training duties)	
Tempy. Wt. Teleg.	†R. D. Dixon.............. 3 July 44	
Wt. Shipwright	...F. E. A. White (act)...... 27 June 44	
	L. Tann.............. 29 Aug 44	
Wt. Engineer	.....F. A. Hitchcock.......... 28 Apr 45	
Tempy. Wt. Elect.	}†H. Fulton.............. 15 Apr 43	
Wt. Writer Offr.	...F. C. Wengradt.......... 6 Nov 42	
Tempy. Wt. Stores Offr.	}L. J. Morris................. 6 Oct 41	
Tempy. Wt. Catering Offr.	A. L. Simons (act)............ 1 Nov 44	
Tempy. Mid., R.N.R.	}W. G. Bell.............. 8 May 44	

†And for duty with submarines.

For Submarines.

Commander	......V. J. H. Van Der Byl, DSC 27 Sept 44	
Lieut.-Com., R.N.R.	{ L. F. L. Hill (act)...... 25 Nov 43 { K. I. M. Owen.......... 25 Mar 44	
Lieutenant	..........G. E. Mugridge, MBE, (ret). — Mar 43 (In lieu of Specialist (T) Officer.)	
	{ E. A. Dussek.......... — Feb 44 { H. R. B. Newton, DSC...... — Apr 44	
Tempy. Lieut., R.N.V.R.	}H. S. White (act)............ 12 July 43	
Lieutenant (E)	.....L. A. Creed, MBE.......... 20 Nov 43	
Sub-Lieut	..........W. M. S. Boyd.............. 24 Apr 44 A. C. Drewe............... 24 Apr 44	
Tempy. Sub-Lieut., R.N.V.R.	}R. A. Cobb .... 14 Feb 44	
Tempy. Sub-Lieut., R.N.Z.N.V.R.	}W. E. Hood.............. — Oct 44	
Tempy. Cd. Gunner	}(T) R. Hague (act)............ 2 July 43	
Cd. Engineer	.....G. Mitchell............... 21 June 43	
Tempy. Mid., R.N.V.R.	}I. H. S. Silver............... 20 Sept 43	

W.R.N.S.

Second Officer	.....G. R. Judge................. 20 Jan 44 (In Charge, W.R.N.S.)	
Third Officer	...F. E. Taylor............... 3 Mar 45	
Act. Third Officer	.R. Moore.............. 26 Nov 44 A. C. M. Hunter............. 25 Mar 45	

CYGNET.

Lieut.-Com. R.N.R.	}A. H. Pierce, OBE (act)...... 30 June 45	
Lieutenant	.........E. V. Bezance............... 14 Oct 44 D. W. Napper............... — May 45	
Lieutenant, R.N.R.	}R. B. Mann.............. 26 June 45	
Tempy. Lieut., R.N.V.R.	}W. J. A. Bryce............. — Dec 43	
Tempy. Surg.-Lieut., R.N.V.R.	}R. G. Whitelaw, MB, CHB 8 July 44	
Tempy. Sub-Lieut., R.N.V.R.	{ P. A. Leworthy.............. 10 June 43 { A. R. Byford.............. 4 July 44 { A. G. Heffer............. 16 July 44	
Cd. Engineer	.....W. M. Jones............ 29 Nov 43	

CYNTHIA.

Tempy. Lieut., R.N.V.R.	{ C. L. Chatwin............... 3 Dec 43 { (In Command) { J. G. Clark............. 19 Oct 44	
Tempy. Sub-Lieut., R.N.V.R.	{ F. B. Marley.............. 1 Dec 43 { J. R. Knighton............ 10 Dec 43 { S. E. Pollett............. 18 Sept 44	
Tempy. Elect. Sub-Lieut., R.N.V.R.	}J. T. J. Lornie............... — Feb 44	

CYPRESS. (Po.)

Tempy. Skipper, R.N.R.	{ W. B. Redepenning......... 25 Feb 44 { (In Command) { R. W. Down .... 20 Sept 44 { W. Ross............. 2 Feb 45	

CYSNE II.

DABCHICK.

Tempy. Lieut.-Com., R.N.R.	}P. E. Martin (act)........ 8 Dec 44 (In Command)	
Tempy. Lieut., S.A.N.F.(V)	}E. C. Buhler................ — June 45	

DACRES.

Commander	..........A. H. Thorold, OBE DSC■ 16 Apr 45 (In Command of 15th Escort Group)	
Lieutenant	.........R. S. Beveridge.......... 12 Apr 45 (In Command) T. L. Davies.......... 14 Dec 43	
Tempy. Lieut., R.N.V.R.	{ F. Parr.......... 8 Feb 45 { G. A. B. Stewart (act)...... — Sept 44	
Tempy. Lieut. (E), R.N.R.	}F. A. Kelly, MBE......... 4 Mar 45	
Tempy. Sub-Lieut., R.N.R.	}E. A. Reaves................ 28 Aug 43	
Tempy. Sub-Lieut., R.N.V.R.	}A. Marshall................. 18 Feb 45	
Tempy. Act. Sub-Lieut., R.N.V.R.	}D. G. Wargent............ — July 43	
Tempy. Sub-Lieut. (E), R.N.V.R.	}D. Simpson............. 4 Mar 45	

DAEDALUS.

Vice Admiral	......D. W. Boyd, CB, CBE, DSC 1 June 45 (Flag Officer, Naval Air Stations.)	

	Personal Staff	
Admiral's Secretary	}Commander (S) A. G. Sowman......... 1 June 45	
Asst. Secretary	...Lieut.-Com. (S) T. P. Gillespie, MBE (act)....... 1 May 45	
Flag Com.	..........F. W. B. Edwards.......... 11 June 45	

	Staff.	
Chief Staff Offr.	}Captain W. T. Couchman, DSO, OBE................. 30 May 43	
Secretary	.............Lieutenant (S) R. W. Kego 26 Mar 45	
Captain	..............Lord Ailwyn (act) (ret)...... 23 July 43 (Administration Captain.)	
Captain	..............C. J. N. Atkinson......... — Jan 44 (Training Captain). D. B. Nichol (act)......... 22 Aug 44 (Maintenance Captain) J. S. Baker (act) (ret) ...... 8 Nov 43 J. V. Findlay (act) .... 22 Aug 44	

Tempy. Elect. Sub-Lieut., R.N.V.R.	P. E. Collis (proby)	6 Oct 43
	G. Gledhill	25 Oct 43
	H. V. Shanklin	28 Dec 43
	O. S. Steele (proby)	14 Aug 44
Tempy. Sub-Lieut. (S), R.N.V.R.	R. V. Deacon	19 Aug 43
Tempy. Lieut. (Sp. Br.), R.N.V.R.	C. J. Byrne	27 Dec 43
Tempy. Sub-Lieut. (Sp. Br.) R.N.V.R.	C. H. Markham	6 Dec 43
	W. H. Blunt	26 Oct 43
Tempy. Wt. Engineer	H. L. Champion	4 Aug 44
Chief Shipper, R.N.R.	G. Hughes (act)	5 Oct 43
Tempy. Skipper, R.N.R.	T. Buchan	16 May 43
	W. E. Nightingale	7 June 43
	R. S. G. Hicks	5 Oct 43

W.R.N.S.

Second Officer	A. C. Heath	17 May 44
	E. Noble	5 Oct 44

ISKRA.

Lieut.-Com.	R. H. Thornton (emgcy)	— June 43
	(In Command)	
Tempy. Lieut. (E)	T. P. G. Brown	20 Mar 44
Tempy. Lieut. (E), R.N.V.R.	E. F. Osborne	19 Mar 44
Tempy. Sub-Lieut., R.N.V.R.	D. H. Wallington	23 Aug 43
	H. Rayner	29 Feb 44
Tempy. Mid., R.N.V.R.	P. B. Johnson	4 Aug 44

ISLANDA.

ISLAY.

Skipper Lieut. R.N.R.	O. Jinks (act)	— Sept 43
	(In Command)	
Tempy. Skipper, R.N.R.	H. G. M. Krause	21 Sept 44
	J. W. Moore	24 Mar 43
	T. C. Whitcombe	— Apr 44

ISLE OF GUERNSEY.

Tempy. Lieut. (E), R.N.R.	A. J. Hatcher	16 Nov 42

ISLE OF MAY.

Tempy. Lieut., R.N.V.R.	E. C. O. M. Raymond	8 Mar 43
	(In Command.)	

ISLE OF SARK.

Commander	G. L. Bodoano (act)	30 Dec 44
	(In Command)	
Lieutenant, R.N.R.	(N*) P. R. Lewis	19 Feb 44

Tempy. Lieut., R.N.V.R.	C. E. Turner	20 Oct 43
	F. J. Perks	— May 44
	F. N. Beaney	18 Oct 43
Tempy. Lieut. Com. (E), R.N.R.	F. L. C Miller	20 Aug 43
Tempy. Lieut. (E), R.N.R.	J. Wilson	18 Dec 43
Tempy Sub-Lieut., R.N.V.R.	H. W. Fleetwood	1 Nov 43
Tempy. Sub-Lieut. (E), R.N.R.	A. B. Auld	19 Jan 44
Tempy. Act. Sub-Lieut. (E), R.N.V.R.	W. D. Barnes	12 Jan 44
	M. J. Patman	29 Feb 44
	L. H. Ryman	7 Dec 43
	W. D. H. Houghton	9 Oct 44
	F. W. Whiter	9 Oct 44
Tempy. Act. Sub-Lieut. (S), R.N.V.R.	A. W. Lovell	— Dec 44
Tempy. Sub-Lieut. (Sp. Br.), R.N.V.R.	I. S. Cumming	3 Mar 44

ISLE OF THANET.

Tempy. Lieut. Com. (E), R.N.R.	A. W. Husband	29 May 42
Tempy. Lieut. (E), R.N.R.	J. F. Bell	7 July 42
Tempy. Surg.-Lieut., R.N.V.R.	H. F. Bateman, MB, Bch.	16 Oct 44
Tempy. Sub-Lieut., R.N.Z.N.V.R.	A. G. Grimson	9 May 42
Tempy. Act. Sub-Lieut.(E) R.N.V.R.	R. Bowers	25 May 42

ISTRIA.

Skipper Lieut. R.N.R.	A. E. Larner (act)	17 Aug 43
	(In Command)	
Tempy. Skipper, R.N.R.	J. W. Nicol	3 Dec 43
	T. E. J. Neve	21 Nov 44

ITHURIEL.

Lieutenant (E)	N. H. Card (act)	12 May 44
Tempy. Gunner	(T) A. J. Lloyd	15 Dec 43

JACANA.

Tempy. Lieut., R.N.V.R.	R. L. Harris	27 Nov 44
	(In Command)	

JACINTA.

Tempy. Lieut., R.N.V.R.	A. L. Boyde	23 Nov 44
	(In Command)	
	J. Priestley	9 Dec 43
Tempy. Gunner	(T) A. E. Meadus	9 Dec 43

HMS Drake (Vicarage Road Camp)

I can no longer recall if we did joining routine at RNB and were transferred to Vicarage Road Camp or went straight there from HMFDT-13, in any event this Camp was a new one to us having just been released to the RN from use by the US Navy.

The origins of the Camp went back to 1925 when it was called 'Vicarage Gardens Camp', or 'White City' by the locals; then it was attached to HMS Vivid for the purpose of training Cooks, Stokers and Writers plus others. It was situated on steeply sloping ground close to Brunell's famous railway bridge of tubular construction crossing the Tamar and just round Bull Point from St. Budeaux Camp.

Accommodation, much expanded for WW2, was some one hundred and twenty Nissen and sectional wooden huts of the traditional military style and what we met was a considerable eye-opener to all, used to the frugal and Spartan ways of the RN and did morale no good whatsoever for, when moving out, the US Navy had left behind a veritable cornucopia which, on inspection, appeared to be most of their equipment.

The galley was full of food, all the fridges stuffed with goodies not seen for years; the tailors shop full of uniforms of every conceivable type and even the sewing machines were still in place.

Scattered inside and outside the huts was ammunition of all descriptions and in my locker there was a Garand with the trigger guard bashed in.

Every bunk had a bedside light and almost all had an electric toaster, put to immediate good use and we nearly lived on toast and butter until the Top Brass heard about it all and confiscated them.

Every hut had a large paraffin heater, some had two, and copious supplies to keep them fueled but again, when word of this lavish lifestyle filtered through to the Top Brass they had them removed and we relapsed to living as approved by King's Regulations and Admiralty Instructions, little changed from the days of the Wooden Walls, how Nelson would have been proud of it all.

Little of this profusion went to waste, most of the draft kitted themselves out with the finest quality US Navy gear, and fine it was too compared with ours; I suppose all the guns and ammo were collected up together with the heaters, toasters and bedside lights and anything else lying around that did not conform to Good Order and Naval Discipline.

Out of all this profligate abundance I managed to hang on to a US Navy hand axe which I still have to this day.

Of the personnel in the Camp there appeared to be a considerable scattering from all around the RN, even some Fleet Air Arm which was most unusual, and life was very relaxed there for some time.

We mounted our own guards and in general ran the Camp ourselves; for my part most of the time seemed to be spent washing up, a valuable experience for later life tho' how long this haven of peace and tranquility lasted I no longer remember but in due course the Camp closed and we were all packed off back to RNB sometime about December 1945, so I suppose it was Christmas in RNB.

Bull Point, Devonport;
Vicarage Road Camp and St. Budeaux Camp.

HMS Newcastle

P arading in the Drill Sheds with my worldly goods (naval) around me together with an assorted bunch of hopefuls for scattering *en route* to the Far East, I prepared to join Newcastle in the Dockyard at Devonport.

HMS Newcastle was a Southampton Class cruiser of some 9,100 tons built by Vickers Armstrong on the Tyne in 1936 and with a crew of 830.

The Captain at the time was A.F. St.G. Orpen OBE, DSC and a staff of thirty officers; there was a Commodore aboard too but he was probably in transit.

We must have got under weigh quite smartly with the draft being variously distributed among the ship's company depending on trades for working ship so I found myself doing watches on the bridge, messenger, lookout and that sort of valuable contribution.

Crossing the Bay of Biscay we must have been in a hurry tho' just why was a mystery as the war was now well and truly over; it was rough and there was considerable 'slamming', (*i.e*: the bows would come out of the water and then fall with a great crash), shaking the whole ship and as it dug into the next wave the stern would come out of the water and the props would revv freely....wump,wump,wump.wump...then CRASH as the bows fell again; this is where hammocks came into their own.

For Middle and Morning Watches we mustered on the iron deck amidships very close to the bakery which emitted a tantalising smell of baking bread, appetising at the best of times but under these condition leading to a state of near desperation; now, when I smell baking bread, I am transported back instantly to HMS Newcastle in the bitter miserable cold of a wet heaving deck in the middle of the night.

HMS Newcastle in harbour at Devonport

HMS Newcastle entering Grand Harbour, Malta

First call was Gibraltar to drop some of the draft off and pick up others; we had a run ashore but I remember nothing of it; next stop was Malta only four months after the visit aboard FDT-13;we anchored in Grand Harbour and I had an early shore leave; in this case the side gangway had not yet been rigged so we were obliged to use the boom; shock, horror, this was a wooden pole about thirty feet long and about ten inches diameter at right angles to the side of the ship and along which one inched towards a rope ladder dangling from the end, down which one descended in the approved manner into the heaving liberty boat at the bottom; one slip and you were in the drink. All this was fine for the proper sailors of pre war times but for HOs a tricky business.

The rest of the time in Valetta was spent painting ship, (again), in this case my bit was a part of the bows which had a very considerable overhang thus trying to dab on paint at more than arm's length whilst dangling on a short piece of board and suspended by a single rope was a bit difficult to say the least.

I do not think we stopped off at Port Said but continued thro' the Suez Canal and dropped anchor off Aden; there was no shore leave as Nationalist rumblings were getting louder and it was decidedly unhealthy being British; we did take on personnel from the Persian Gulf and I remember thinking how brown they all were compared with us pallid specimens; many of them ended up in 5 Mess at Bambara with me and we became good friends.

By now I had struck up a friendship with some of the ships radar operators and had a guided tour round the Warning sets;Newcastle had Types 281 and 271; this latter was the usual prefabricated unit above and behind the gunnery director and reached by a rather perilous ladder welded up the side; the set had a PPI and automatic aerial rotation.

I got very keen on all this and approached the ship's radar officer to see if he could get me transferred from the draft to ship's company as they were short of an operator but this was not possible so I continued on to Ceylon. Some two and a half weeks had gone by and Newcastle was approaching India with Bombay our next call; we docked alongside and dropped off a draft but there was no shore leave.

It looked dry and dusty and it was very hot;we had travelled some seven thousand five hundred miles since leaving UK and had another thousand to do so we slipped out of the harbour *en route* for Columbo, Ceylon.

January 21st saw us leave Newcastle, it had taken about three weeks to do the eight and a half thousand miles so deleting some five days for stops we had sailed some five hundred and fifty miles per twenty four hours thus giving an average speed of well over twenty knots.

There was not a single incident on the journey that gave any indications of danger,in fact the only time this did happen was on FDT-13 where a free floating mine was spotted in the Mediterranean so one of the Starboard Oerlikons was closed up and proceeded to plaster it, aided by pistol brandishing officers on the bridge; the pesky thing did not explode so I suppose it sank.

Taking leave of Newcastle, gleaming in the hot sun, I never saw her again tho' she was in Trinco on one occasion when I was at Bambara; their Lordships must have thought her worth saving as she had a major overhaul and 'my' radar was replaced by more modern stuff.

Anno domini got her in the end and she was scrapped at Faslane in 1959.

HMS Mayina

Originally Chatham Camp and administered by that Port Division it became HMS Mayina (it means 'bird' in Sinhalese) on 1st January 1945; this did not last long as it became HMS Gould on 31st March 1946 as the base of the Pacific Fleet previously located in Australia. The Camp was situated close to the village of Kelenia some five miles north of Columbo and started life as a tea plantation.

On 7th March 1946 almost the whole of the Camp was burnt to the ground, an easy matter with the palm leaf Bhandas, for reasons indeterminate but either Ceylon Nationalists or disgruntled Matloes with a demob grudge, or even,tho' unlikely, a mere accident; my Service Certificate suggests that I was there at the time but is evidently in error as one could hardly miss an event of that magnitude, possibly I was in transit and on Mayinas books.

The establishment was of substantial size; the Commanding Officer was Captain W.R.G. Reid RN with a staff of fifty three officers plus twenty officers 'for destroyers' and a further five hundred 'for disposal'.

The original planters house now housed the Sick Bay and there were one or two other fairly permanent buildings but all the rest were Bhandas.

First job immediately after arriving at Mayina was an issue of tropical clothing and this took the form of long khaki trousers and battledress tops in some sort of Aertex material; these fitted mainly where they touched, generally the shoulders and there were some astonishing sights until the Camp tailors got to work.

Added to the usual joining routine was a bevvy of vaccinations and inoculations, jabs in each arm as one walked past the Medical Staff; black water

HMS Mayina

fever, yellow fever and sundry other horrors spring to mind and there were quite a few adverse reactions with some being quite ill.

We were also introduced to an anti malarial drug, either Atebrin or Mepacrine and it turned the recipient a jaundiced yellow but seemed to work as I never heard of any cases of malaria.

Ceylon really was a foreign land, tropical weather, dark skinned people and so forth; for the first two nights tom toms played incessantly for some funeral rites in Kelenia and to add further to our musical entertainment there was a rating with a serious Caruso complex and he inflicted Jerusalem on us, *fortissimo,* until every piece of glass within miles was shattered. Everyone was very edgy with the Ceylon Nationalists stirring up anti-British feeling and, from time to time taking direct action; one consequence of this was going to the heads at night when you had to be extra careful and announce intentions to the sentry, many of whom were armed with Lanchester sub-machine guns and a burst of fire could easily come your way with very detrimental results.

One night after the liberty boat had returned a shot was heard and a vast rumpus ensued; it seems that a well known Scot, ex-Glasgow razor gangs had returned and felt the need for food thus made a tentative raid on the galley; however a messmate was on guard and noting the refusal of said Scot to take advice was obliged to shoot him in the leg thus rendering him immobile; by the time the Court Martial came up we had long since left so never heard the outcome.

I had struck up a friendship with an SBA (sick bay attendant) and together we had several runs ashore, visiting most of the interesting spots including Mount Lavinia where we went swimming on occasions; this was one of the more holy places of Empire which was now very much on the wane.

By now I had been allocated a job, that of 'server' on the ratings mess-deck, actually a row of tables outside the galley, and there I collected the food from said galley and took it to the tables; there was a spin-off from this in that, being 'in' with the Cooks meant a decided benefit so far as personal catering was concerned.

Being a transit camp few remained very long and about the end of March we paraded outside the guard room with kit and baggage for onward transport to HMS Bambara, effected via the medium of Ceylon Railways.

It is some one hundred and sixty miles from Columbo to Trincomalee, across the width of the island and the railway wound through some very spectacular scenery, across the jungle clad plains and up into the mountain passes.

The seats were slatted wood and very uncomfortable in the hot sultry conditions and a visit to the toilet interesting as this item consisted of a brass lined funnel in the floor and a couple of handles to hang on to. Body and soul were kept together on this long journey by K Rations, a complete meal in a small cardboard box, down to a fag and matches and a couple of pieces of toilet paper; naturally it was American.

It took a long time to get across the island with innumerable stops but eventually we ground to a halt at China Bay Halt and through the trees appeared the flat open expanse of an airfield, RNAS Trincomalee, otherwise HMS Bambara, our home for some unknown time to come.

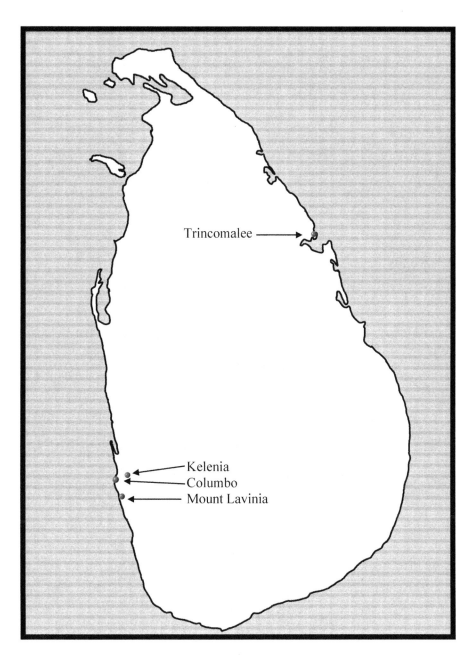

Sketch Map of Ceylon

CERTIFICATE FOR WOUNDS AND HURTS

These are to Certify the Right Honourable the Lords Commissioners of the Admiralty that

(Name in full) (Rank or Rating) (Official Number)

HILTON. J   S. B. A.   D/MX.109827

belonging to His Majesty's Ship "Mayina"

was *injured, on 7th March 19 46 as shown on the reverse hereof,

and that I/we, having enquired into the circumstances in which he received the † injury stated, and having heard the evidence of

(Insert Name and Rank or Rating)

who witnessed the accident, consider that he was then actually On His Majesty's Service in that he receive the burns described overleaf, as the result of a fire which occurred at H.M.S. "Mayina" on 7th March, 1946

* "Injured" or "Wounded"

† "Injury" or "Wound"

Here describe the manner in which the injury was received and also the particular act of duty or form of physical recreation in which it was incurred as required by Article 1419 of the King's Regulations.

¯Delete when case is investigated by Captain.

Signatures and Ranks of Investigating Officers.

Signature of Officer or Man injured

Date 19 Signature of Captain

H.M.S. Mayina

73

NOTE: The grant of a Hurt Certificate to a Petty Officer or Man is to be noted on his Service Certificate and in the Ships Ledger.

Report of Wound or Hurt.

(Name in full.)   *(Rank or Rating)*   *(Official Number)*

HINTON. J   S.P.h.   D/LX.109827

belonging to His Majesty's Ship   "Loyina"

sustained the following injury on 7th March 19 46

"Injury" or "Wound"

2nd Degree burns of back and arms.

Here describe minutely the nature of the injury sustained as required by Article 1419 of the King's Regulations

Personal Description

Age about 21 years. Born at or near Worcester.
Height 6ft –ins. Hair Fair Eyes blue Complexion pale.

Particular Marks or Scars

Mole above (R) eyebrow.

Date 13ᵗʰ March 1946   Signature of Medical Officer

To be completed if Hurt Certificate (overleaf) is **NOT** awarded

"Officer" or "Man"

"Injury" or "Wound"

I/we, having enquired into the circumstances in which the above named sustained the stated, and having heard the evidence of

(Insert Name and Rank or Rating)

who witnessed the accident, consider that he was **not** at the time On His Majesty's Service.

Delete when case is investigated by Captain.

Signatures and Ranks of Investigating Officers.

Signature of Officer or Man injured

Date 19   Signature of Captain   74

H.M.S.

Part 2

Bambara

HMS Bambara

As appropriate to an airbase Bambara translates as 'wasp' in Sinhalese and was the ship's name for Royal Naval Air Station Trincomalee or RNAS (T). It had been an RAF airfield with a strong Fleet Air Arm (FAA) element, all substantially built in brick according to the architectural styles of the times and then known as RAF China Bay and opening in November 1939.

It was handed over to the FAA on November 1st 1944 for use as an RN Aircraft Maintenance Base and became operational on November 15th that year; it reverted to the RAF after the RN moved out and in 1957 was handed over to the Royal Ceylon Air Force; now the Sri Lanka Air Force.

It was a very large establishment in terms of manpower as well as acreage, listed availability of accommodation was for 390 officers, 3,900 Chiefs, Petty Officers and ratings plus 12 Wrn officers and 100 ratings; by the time we arrived those large numbers had declined somewhat and must have approximated to 2,000 or so.

Commanding Officer was Captain H.W.S. Browning DSO, OBE and the Commander Cdr. O.S. Stevinson, the terror of the ship, together with some 133 officers. Having detrained at China Bay Halt we queued in the usual way outside the Divisional Office for allocation of messes and so forth when a praying mantis, vivid green and of vast proportions landed on one of the party, it was a sign of the times and there was immediate panic.

When calm had been restored the typists and drivers were filtered from the mob; drivers in particular were very scarce, Britain was not then the car owning society it later became and out of the draft there was only one, Prickett, an ex-barber who went on to great things driving one of the fire engines; typists likewise were scarce and an interesting oddity was that the Commanders' typist was always, by some obscure Naval tradition, from the Seaman branch.

Most of us were billetted at Natchykanda Camp so the next move was to find where this lay on the sprawling vastness of the base and get ourselves and kit over there.

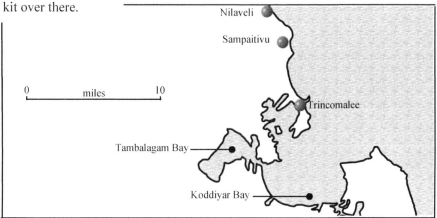

Natchykanda Camp

Ike Elkins, fellow RP3 and oppo elected to get ourselves to Natch. (as it was called), by independent means unaware that there was transport available all around the base. So, humping our hammocks and kit bags, set off in the 100°F plus at mid-day and, after walking some considerable distance, found ourselves at Clappenburg Bay, the aircraft overhaul facility, to discover that we had been walking the wrong way so waited for suitable transport to rescue us and this turned out to be a ten ton Mack doing a regular bus service; we hopped gratefully aboard *en route* for Natch.

The camp was situated on a promontory that protruded into Tambalagam Bay, itself an almost landlocked bay of the Inner Harbour.

The camp consisted of some fifty Bhanda type huts and I suppose there were messing facilities and admin. offices available but I cannot recall details. This was the second taste of accommodation in the tropics and something of a novelty in that there were palm trees all around, lush vegetation and almost surrounded by the sea, a mini paradise indeed even if we did waken in the mornings to find the bedding streaked with blood (ours) from the squashed bed bugs which emerged from the bed springs during the night for a free meal; their careers cut very short by a blow lamp. Flying insects, of which there was a vast profusion, some friendly and others definitely not,were kept largely at bay with mosquito nets.

Space per person was the standard metal framed bed to accommodate hammocks plus a wooden locker for kit or such that would fit into it so, suitably accommodated,we set off to look for the radar set we had been sent all this way, at great cost, to operate.

As luck would have it the set was installed not all that far away on the other side of the threshold of runway 06 close to a coconut grove; it was an Army set, probably a GL3 and the usual mobile arrangement of generator and set on separate trailers, the set in a rotatable cabin containing the transmitter and receiver plus the aerial on the side and top of the cabin. The whole thing buzzed and hummed with life but no-one wsas watching the trace as all the crew were outside in the sun playing whist as tho' their lived depended on it, a trait that continued all thro' the ADR (Air Direction Room), the mess, the W/T (Wireless & Telegraphy) room and possibly the toilets too; maybe they are still playing to this day; Lofty Ford are you there?

We could not have been very long at Natch. when a draft arrived sending most of us to HMS Ausonia, anchored in the Inner Harbour; so much for being radar operators, clearly there had been a change of plans, at least for the time being; it must have been about the middle of April 1946.

TRINCOMALEE

Date of Original. 21.5.44

79

HMS Ausonia

In retrospect it was discovered that the radar set has gone u/s and was not to be repaired so there was no need for operators, so much for sending us to Bambara; Ausonia was in some way attached to Bambara and must have been a dumping ground as there was no clear need for our presence aboard.

Ausonia was built in 1921 by Armstrong Whitworths at Newcastle for Cunard for their Canadian passenger run and displaced some 21,000 tons; she was one of a similar group of such ships; Alaunia, aboard which I was briefly involved; Antonia, Aurania and Ascania, all of which became Armed Merchant Cruisers (AMC's) for the RN, some variously being renamed.

Ausonia was impressed by the Admiralty at the outbreak of WW2 in 1939 and was converted to an AMC for operation with the Atlantic convoys as a part of the Halifax Escort Group.

This continued until 1942 when she was withdrawn for conversion to a Heavy Repair Ship and was in such a guise when I boarded her at Trincomalee where she had been since arrival in 1944, the Admiralty having purchased her outright at that date but after the war she was laid up until 1957 when she was taken out of reserve, refitted and continued in use as a Depot Ship then a Base Heavy Repair Ship in various parts of the World.

Finally paying off in 1964 she went to Spain for scrapping in 1965; an unusually long life but more than likely due to her semi static role.

She was anchored in the Inner Harbour close to HMS Highflyer, the shore base, it was rumoured that Ausonia would never get to sea again due to the vast pile of gash reputed to have piled up underneath her.

The stay on board was very uncomfortable, it was very overcrowded and extremely hot, sleeping below deck was difficult and most slept on the open decks where the temperature was bearable.

What little we did aboard was to provide a bit of muscle heaving things around, so much for a years expensive technical training; the work done, as befitting a Heavy Repair Ship, was all sorts of repairs to ships and almost anything in, and on, them; engines, hulls, boilers, guns, radios and so on.

This was the first time I had seen an American radar set and was much impressed with the professional design and layout with superb accessibility for servicing, a bit of a contrast to ours which looked a bit of a rag bag of cables, switches, dials and sundry odds and ends. Work was done on all sorts of smallish ships, trawlers, corvettes, frigates and, on one occasion, a couple of small coastal submarines so I took this opportunity to go aboard to see what the radar set up was like.

Condition were most horrendously cramped and life aboard must have been very hard work indeed; the radar was a Type 291 (which was derived from an RAF 1.5M ASV set) with a high pressure seal for the aerial feed and the lot had been crammed in making life even more difficult for the crew and I soon realised that the draft to FDT 13 had saved me from this or worse.

Maybe it was something in the water but I seemed to spend a great deal of time aboard Ausonia in the rattle, usually occasioned for returning from leave a bit adrift; generally this punishment took the form of washing down paintwork on stand easy, or marching round the crane deck with rifle and pack in the mid-day heat.

You had to be very careful not to do anything contrary to King's Regulations and Admiralty Instructions (KR&AI), in fact almost everything ratings did seemed to be contrary to KR&AIs.

The ship was crewed mainly by technical types, large numbers of Warrant Officers, Chief Pettty Officers (CPOs), and Petty Officer Engine Room Artificers (PO ERAs), Radio Mechs. and the like; Commanding Officer was Captain Hutchinson DSO, CBE with an RNR Commander and some twenty officers. A notable personal event aboard was whilst early morning scrubbing the decks, a vital part of RN lore and ritual, whereby the PO i/c this exercise did not think my scrubbing was worthy of his overseeing and packed me off to become Messdeck Dodger, that is to say, one who had overall control of the state of the messeck, cleaning, tidyness and so forth and this must have been carried out to the satisfaction of all including the Warrant Bosun who thought my Turks Head knots and general fancy ropework to be excellent; this a spin off from interest in bends and hitches, splicing and the like which still comes in handy today.

One day there was a snap inspection of the hammock nettings and many miscreants were found who had not lashed their hammocks in accordance with the Seaman's Manual and KR&AIs so I was given instructions to append a notice in some suitable public gaze to the effect that all offenders were to report to the Officer on Duty for roasting as required by KR&AIs.

This was done by chalking a 'request' on the deck in an attempt to introduce some politeness into RN life, a feature notably lacking, but this did not go down at all well with Higher Authority and I myself was hauled up before the OD who addressed me in Ringing Tones with the observation that life in the RN was 'ordered' or else !

HMS Ausonia

It was clear from this that I would not be able to introduce any politeness in RN life so 'request' was altered to 'ordered' in accordance with KR&AIs. Ausonia was notable for having a CW (Commission and Warrant) rating who rushed about the place being Terribly Keen and Efficient; 'chaps got a White Paper following him around' was the story, actually he was one who had been picked out for a possible commission and must have been a Y Scheme entry much the same as myself, tho' in my case my feet were still firmly on the bottom rung; I wonder what happened to him in the end ?

One chap in the mess was waiting for a Court Martial having been a sentry on a ship of the Royal Indian Navy which was going through a mutiny phase for reasons unknown; emerging on deck late one night he espied a large group of ratings behaving in a very suspicious manner and (so he reasoned) likely mutineers so to forestall hostile action against himself he duly sprayed the group with his Lanchester sub machine gun killing and wounding sundry of them. What the result of the case was we never heard so if anyone out there does know please write and tell me.

I left Ausonia on May 6th.1946 for return to Bambara HQ and was not sorry to go; the next posting would be to Malay Cove Camp.

Malay Cove Camp

Malay Cove, in the days of the RAF, had been the flying boat base for Sunderlands and Catalinas, the wrecks and dismembered relics of which still littered the base and the Camp was the overhaul and accommodation facility; there was a slipway for hauling machines out of the water and two Bellman hangars, now disused.

So far as the RN was concerned Malay Cove Camp was one of the many semi-autonomous camps round the base and used mainly as a transit camp for the British Pacific Fleet and East Indies Fleet plus all the other odds and ends; I was posted there as Staff to join seven others, plus assorted Chief Petty Officers (CPOs) and Petty Officers (POs) and the usual officers, the Commanding Officer (CO) being a Lt. Cdr. RNR.

Most of the buildings were bhandas but some were of more durable construction from RAF days including the Divisional Office where I was sent to work; this was a clerical job and would have been better done by Writers, nevertheless Ike and myself ran it all, checking in and out drafts here and there plus allocating personnel for guard duties, special duties and so on, a position of considerable power, even, on occasion, allowing us to overrule the Officer of the Day at HQ and sometimes that included the formidable Gunnery Officer one Lt. Baker, a course of action not normally to be undertaken lightly.

The exercising of such power by an AB (equivalent to Lance Corporal) was, of course, a bit of a problem but a remedy was soon found to deal with this in that a Petty Officer's cap was displayed in a prominent position and worked like a charm.

In between this activity there was a lot of spare time to roam around the Camp and look at the animal life which abounded; on one occasion there was a great rumpus in the bushes outside and thinking it was an ape of which there was a profusion I threw half a brick in the general direction and to my surprise out rolled a vast Monitor Lizard looking a bit stunned.

It was grey, prehistoric looking and very big so I picked it up by the tail, it must have been over five feet long, and took into the office to show Ike; at this point the lizard came to life in a spectacular manner and proceeded to rampage round the office with Ike and myself perched on the desk tops not too sure of the safety of the animal.

Eventually someone plucked up courage to open the door and it rushed outside to the relief of all.

There was wild life in abundance, Gibbon Apes used to sit on the roofs of the huts and were to be regarded with suspicion as they could be very vicious and were known to attack people, especially alone.

In the evenings large fruit eating bats appeared, Flying Foxes, as large as a crow and, unlike most bats, had very attractive faces.

Lizards of all sorts were everywhere, some about two feet long changed colour from a vivid green to a bright pink with all shades between and, in the huts, little Ghekko lizards chirped away as they wandered across the ceilings and walls aided by large pads on their feet.

RNAS Trincomalee, HMS Bambara (HQ)

Snakes were an ever present threat as many were very poisonous and best to avoid them if given a chance as was the position with the spiders and large black scorpions; of the smaller orders there was a magnificent profusion; from time to time during the breeding season huge hoards would invade the staff bhanda despite all the screening and were dispatched with sprays, the resulting corpses being swept up into piles; flying ants would also materialise at the appointed times and dump their wings in heaps that were a source of wonder.

There were also Elephants and they used to wander onto the runways from time to time causing great confusion; also a suspicion of leopards, some close to the sentry posts thus making that job very unpopular.

At nights, amid the general uproar of insects all around, ghostly fireflies flitted among the trees, their greenish yellow lights twinkling like tiny lamps; what a disappointment to find just a small rather ugly brown beetle. Catering at Malay Cove was 'in house' the galley also being a bhanda with the attendant fire risk and there was also a small canteen dispensing little other than Pilsener Lager in metal containers a bit like metal polish tins, most people kept a small crate of the stuff under their bunks; we even had a library, I recall it well as one day in there reading a book everything doubled itself in a very sinister fashion to be followed rapidly by a bout of Dengue fever so I wasted in bed for a few days feeling very ill indeed while it passed; it could have been malaria with all the future problems so at least I was spared that.

Large numbers of personnel had, by now, been returned to UK for demob. and this was the bulk of our work; in time it was decided that the Divisional Office was surplus so the Regulating Office next door did both jobs and we moved there for a bit; recreation was scant, there was a cinema at Bambara which ran all the popular films where we could escape reality for a bit, also some way down the Trinco road and close to the threshold of runway 24 stood a local legend in the form of a canteen called 'Kate Kearneys'. It was a sort of civvy forces canteen in the form of a monster bhanda run by the local European ladies for the benefit of us oppressed matloes, it supplied light meals and so forth and offered a retreat from bellowing Petty Officers and a relaxation from King's Regulations and Admiralty Instructions; I did not meet Kate that I was aware of, she was reputed to be very old tho' she did have a Pekinese dog that was frequently in attendance and usually made sexual advances to any handy leg. To all those ladies who no doubt gave their spare time for nothing to help us along a bit, a big Thank You.

Other recreation around the airfield, apart from swimming, was paddling about Malay Cove in ex-Walrus wingtip floats converted by cutting a suitable piece off the top, pinching sails and paddles from aircraft survival gear and generally having an enjoyable time paddling and sailing, once directional problems had been overcome but by now time was running out for Malay Cove Camp, most personnel had left for the UK and eventually orders came for us to move to HQ as the Camp was due to close shortly.

We were saddened to leave this comparative haven of peace to move to a super Pusser establishment, we had had our own little world untroubled by higher authority so long as we did our jobs correctly.

It must have been the middle or end of 1946 so back to Bambara HQ.

Old Divisional Office

MALAY COVE WARDROOM
TRINCOMALEE

5 Cents

Book No. A 362

Available for two months from date of issue.

New Divisional and Regulating Offices

Staff Bhanda

Flying Control

With the closing of Malay Cove Camp I returned to HQ as formal Ship's Company and was allocated to Number 5 Mess, B. Block; as yet no job had been found for me tho' it soon would and further, it might not be to my liking, so I would have to move rapidly.

All along,with an intense interest in aeroplanes and radio I had had an eye on the Control Tower which dealt with both and better still, was attached to the Fleet Air Arm (FAA) thus divorcing me from the RN proper and obvious advantages with regard to working conditions, Special Duty status and so on; this progress was aided by the knowledge that a new arrival in the Mess was drafted especially to work in the Tower; salvation was at hand so I went down to the Tower and spoke to the Senior Flying Control Officer, one Lt. Mahoney, busy packing his gear for home; he proved to be a very decent chap to the extent of asking if there was anything I would like taking to the UK as he had a bit of spare space.

I explained the situation, I was a dab hand at radios, knew all about aeroplanes, was a radar operator with knowledge of Fighter Direction techniques and fluent in R/T, far better than the chap allocated and so forth; it worked and I got the job, probably on the basis that one volunteer was better than ten pressed men.

When I reported for duty it was to be in the ADR (Air Direction Room) as a Fighter Direction Officer (FDO) operating what today would be called 'Approach Control' and dealing with movements over a large part of Ceylon.

The callsign was 'Trinco' but there was a problem, nothing worked as someone had put a pick through the main cables leading to the transmitter block and no-one knew for sure where the damage was so frantic digging took place

JBL on Main Hangar

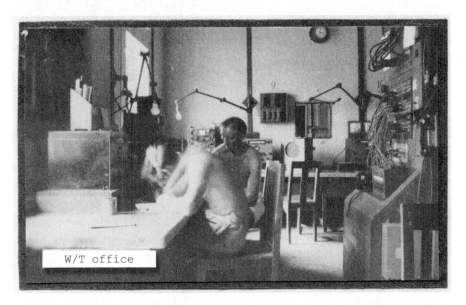

W/T office

In the meantime only Trinco Tower was available on a standby TR1132 set borrowed from a Seafire.

The ADR was an office in the buildings attached to the airfield side of the main hangar, the Main Air Display Plot (MADP) was one side and the W/T office the other with the callsign of 'MHV'.

As FDOs we had intercom contact with almost everyone on the airfield including the VHF/DF at the far end of the field, callsign 'Trinco Homer'.

I recall there were three of us doing this job, Ike Elkins, Minnie Moorehouse and myself and we dealt with all relevant radio calls logging Transmission (Tx) and Reception (Rx). and introduction to the systems of the ADR was brief and basic; "There's the loudspeaker, headsets, telephone, mike, intercom switches and log book plus a large map of Ceylon under a Perspex cover; now get on with it".

JBL and Minnie Moorhouse

So get on with it I did and became an almost instant Able Seaman FDO thereby saving the hard pressed taxpayer a good deal of money in wages.

The resident squadron was 733 equipped mainly with Seafires and had a Canadian pilot who insisted on switching off his radio immediately he had cleared the airfield limits; one day he took off as usual, flew away and did not return within his known endurance so clearly something untoward had happened; had he made a Mayday call VHF/DF might have got a bearing on him but this was not the case so no-one had the faintest idea where he might be except that he would be over land so a

90

sea search would not be necessary; however even a small land search over Ceylon with the dense jungle was a formidable undertaking and all home based aircraft were aloft looking for him.

The problem was not helped by quite large numbers of wrecks already scattered liberally around so aircraft from the carrier Glory, c/s Tophat, in the harbour, were pressed into service, c/s Cooler Aircraft.

The C in C himself came into the office during the search, the closest I ever got to an Admiral whilst in the RN.

In the end it was the specially equipped Jeeps of Search and Rescue, VHF callsign 'Caravan W/T, P2N' who found him after some ten days searching thanks, it was said, to the assistance of the local tribesmen.

Land Search & Rescue ('Caravan')

It was evident that there had been an engine failure and the machine crashed into the jungle killing the pilot on impact; I well recall the signal "body decomposed and shapeless, suggest immediate burial" though what the exact problems were with the engine were never discovered as it was impractical to recover it.

Whilst on duty in the ADR one day I had my sole conversation with the Captain of Bambara, normally a God like Person, quite unreachable to lowly people like myself; on this occasion I was on duty in the ADR listening to the

JBL at Plotting Board in ADR

HMS Glory

radio and swotting a book on radio theory for a City & Guilds course in Telecommunictions Engineering when the August Personage suddenly appeared flanked by the usual crowd of Lesser Persons, no doubt doing some sort of snap inspection.

I sat to attention as directed by KR & AIs (Kings Regulations and Admiralty Regulations), "What was I reading?" enquired the Captain, "I'm reading a book on radio theory sir", I observed.

"Not the book, my man," he said testily, "what frequency are you reading?" It would never have happened with an RNVR officer.

After some time at the ADR word came from on high that I was to transfer to the Tower so the next week was spent writing a book on the myriad systems for my successor; thereafter I packed my bags and took up position in the Tower some couple of hundred yards away.

This was an RAF construction to specification 1959/34, generally referred to as a 'Fort Type' on account of the shape but in this case there was an extra bit added to the top tho' it was never used in my time.

The Tower was the centre of activities on the airfield, containing the offices of Commander Flying, SFCO, Communications Room and the operating position for airfield control on the first floor.

Each day going on duty I wrote up on the Ceylon Airfields Board the serviceability state; there were originally about eight, but by then most were u/s and badly overgrown except Vavunia.

Staff consisted, so far as I recall, of Commander Flying, SFCO and three FCOs one of whom, Lt. Kenny, was our Divisional Officer.

Most FCOs appeared to be failed pilots for one reason or another and some of the training was put to good use in this manner and they were supported by about three ratings like myself.

JBL on duty at 'Trinco' (Approach Control)

There was also a Crash and Rescue Section led by Petty Officer Wells with some six ratings, Scouse Larsen and Mathis are the only names I can now remember; there were also the Hill twins as Runway Controllers suddenly deemed necessary by their Lordships to try to control the worst lunacies on the runways and airfield by rogue pilots.

The Tower equipment was somewhat basic; pressures, which were rarely asked for, were read off an old altimeter kept on the bench and as the airfield was almost sea level and the tower about twenty feet there was less than one mb. between QNH and QFE.

There was a spare TR1132 from a Seafire for use when the main transmitter went u/s, which seemed to be quite often plus a battery operated receiver to check if the airfield beacon was working, callsign 'TM'.

The whole lot was finished off with a Tannoy speaker and hand mike for the R/T, a couple of Aldis Lamps with red and green filters, frequently used, a Very Pistol with an assortment of different coloured cartridges, also frequently used plus smoke puffs for assessing the wind speed and direction and the inevitable log book; with that lot we went to work.

The callsign was 'Trinco Tower' on about 118 m/cs and most of the aircraft were fitted with the standard TR1132 transmitter/receiver with some six crystal controlled frequencies, the pilot having a small control box with appropriate buttons to select the required frequency: "Press button Charlie and call Trinco Homer" would be a typical example.

Sometimes there were odd effects to the VHF signal with ducting and skipping due to temperature inversions and so forth thereby extending the range many times, somewhat the equivalent of a desert mirage and I recall working the RAF flying boat base at the southern end of Ceylon under those conditions, a welcome change from the routine stuff.

Radio workshops; there were too on the airfield, callsign 'Anklet' and the Test Pilot, frequently driven to distraction by no response from the Tower would

Air Sea Rescue ('Moushold')

call them instead; they would then ring for instructions and relay the gen to the pilot; things were, indeed, a bit basic.

Day to day activities were the sort of thing expected on a FAA base, the Seafires of 733 Squadron provided the bulk of work followed closely by Avengers and Fireflies and then a considerable scattering of all sorts; there was the ASR Walrus, notable for the amazing din when it revved up for take off, later to be replaced by a Sea Otter.

There was a story going the rounds that one intrepid pilot had looped a Walrus but to be much discomfited by a hail of ammo. drums for the Vickers K promptly going thro' the prop, a pusher in the Walrus.

Dakotas would come and go mainly bearing VIPs of which there appeared to be a constant stream; on an occasion one appeared to collect the bodies of American servicemen buried locally, the machine being specially fitted out for the bulk carrying of coffins and with a crew of exhumers aboard.

Trinco was a staging post on the long Far East flights and equipped with a Class 2 D/F so there were many calls from Liberators and Yorks engaged on this service, mostly carrying VIPs.

Field Marshall Slim called one day and Lady Mountbatten was a regular visitor all requiring a good deal of blancoing and Honour Guards with the place awash with Top Brass from the C in C downwards.

One day an RAF Mosquito failed to start one engine but elected to take off on Runway 24 for return to Negombo; single engine operation is always hazardous especially at critical speeds, heights and so forth and on this occasion he got to some few hundred feet, lost control, spinning into Tambalagam Bay. Despite the frantic efforts of the duty FCO who raced there in the jeep and dived in fully clothed both crew were dead, probably killed by the impact. The funeral was a few days later and the SFCO thought that I should attend as a representative of the Tower so I was included in the Funeral Firing Party and there was much frantic practice at Arms Reversed and appropriate ceremonials for the event.

They were buried in the service cemetery just outside Trinco; no doubt both crewmen had been through the war and emerged unscathed and to perish at that point seemed less than justice but flying is a hard taskmaster and the slightest lack of concentration can have results out of all proportion. Barracudas from aircraft carriers used Trinco for practice deck landings, ADDLS, on a specially marked out section of the runway to represent the deck of a carrier and many came to grief with the long spindly undercarriage succumbing to the high rate of descent and inexperienced handling.

One hot afternoon, most afternoons were hot, the speaker burst into life with a call from Vavunia Tower, at that point un-occupied for some years. Investigations revealed that Vavunia, more or less central to the island, was being re-opened for the inaugural flight of the recently formed Air Ceylon, and that the eastern terminus for the round the island service would be Trinco and, in due course, a Dakota trundled into the circuit and landed to be met by the Trinco mayor and entourage and large crowd of locals.

Another regular who called up most days for a radio check was Mousehold, the ASR ML sited at some convenient spot in the harbour; I never saw her, nor met any of the crew other than on the radio, tho' she was not needed in my time. The Commander Flying of the carrier Glory had his own private Tiger Moth which he frequently brought over to Trinco doing joyrides and aerobatics; one evening he took off on Runway 06, had an engine failure and was obliged to carry out a forced landing into the harbour, getting very wet and extremely angry in the process.

The investigation showed that the mechanic who filled up the tanks did so from a drum containing the required low(ish) octane fuel and that the drum also contained water, however the mechanic was aware that petrol floated on water and filled the tanks with this in mind tho' what the Commander had to say about a theory of that sort is not recorded.

About July 1947 RAF Squadron 45 arrived with some dozen Beaufighters plus associated ground crews for a stay of several weeks; the aircraft were cannon and rocket equipped for anti shipping and carried out exercises at the range at

Staff of Flying Control

A/C.	Pilots callsign.	Pilot.	Exercise.	Take off.		On Range.	Land.	
B	21	W/C. KEY.	R.P. & Cannon.	09.00	0909	09.10	09.40	0945
Q D	30	F/O. BUGLER.	"	09.00	0947	09.10	09.40	1025
A C J	29	SGT. MITCHELL.	"	09.30	0931	09.40	10.10	1015
J	28	F/O. WOOD.	"	09.30	0926	09.40	10.10	1000
B	23	F/L. BIRBECK.	"	10.00	1013	10.10	10.40	1040
Q D	22	S/L. FOSTER.	"	10.00	1053	10.10	10.40	1141
A C	29	F/O. SAUNDERS	"	10.30		10.40	11.10	
J	25	F/O. BOOKER.	"	10.30	1026	10.40	11.10	1057
B	21	W/C. KEY.	"	11.00	1014	11.10	11.40	
Q D	24	F/O. BINGHAM.	"	11.00	1211	11.10	11.40	
A C	29	SGT. MITCHELL.	"	11.30		11.40	12.10	
J	28	F/O. WOOD.	"	11.30		11.40	12.10	1235

Distribution :

O.C. No.45 Squadron.	Commander Flying H.M.S. Bambara.
Flt. Commander, "	Aerodrome Control Officer "
Armoury "	Air Gunnery Officer, "

(B.H.D. FOSTER)   S/L.,
for Wing Commander,
Commanding No.45 Squadron,
Royal Air Force, Ceylon.

Note: Take off time for the first detail may
be advanced to 0830 hrs.

Nilaveli on the coast some miles north of Trinco so making representations in the right places I got myself a trip on one of these and found it interesting to be on the receiving end of the R/T for a change; rocket attacks required quite a steep approach and the projectiles, when fired, seemed to loaf along under the wings for quite a time until they speeded up and zapped into the target.

Rockets were lethal things giving an aircraft like a Beaufighter the fire power similar to Newcastle and a good deal cheaper.

The airfield had a couple of Lockheed Expeditors used for

Runway Control Van

communications purposes, goodness knows how they got there but they were much used for trips to India and St. Thomas Mount and round the island generally.

Generally they were piloted by a CPO with the radio op. one PO Thomas who claimed that only his high pitched Welsh voice would modulate the HF/RT, the VHF being out of range; it certainly seemed to work.

Out of all the aircraft at Trinco these Expeditors were the only ones to return to UK, all the others were left for whatever fate may have decided for them; perhaps many of them are there to this day.

Life on and around the airfield is worthy of note; the runway was 2400 yards long by the usual narrow Naval 50 yards wide; magnetic headings 06/24.

Only one hangar at HQ was

moderately useable, all the others being destroyed in the April Raids as well as considerable damage to the base generally plus the elderly carrier, Hermes, being sunk in what was a mini Pearl Harbour causing a panic in the local population.

Churchill called this audacious attack "the most dangerous moment" but, very fortunately, the Japs did not attempt landings due to inadequate Army manpower otherwise the results of the war might have been very different. The resident squadron,733,was formed in March 1944 with Seafires and disbanded in Dec.1947 just after Bambara paid off.

In addition there were endless unservicable aircraft scattered all over the airfield, almost all in scrap condition Mosquitos, Albacores, Swordfish,Tiger Moths, Corsairs, Vengences, Masters, Martinets to name but a few and, in Tambalagam Bay at the end of 24, lay the remains of a Liberator from times past but no-one seemed to know the story.

There were drogues for target practice, about the size of a V1 flying bomb; they would swing wildly from side to side during take off and were regarded with grave misgivings.

Working on the airfield produced some benefits as a motor pool was attached to the Tower; a Runway Control Van, Motorcycle, several tractors, jeeps and a small van or two plus fire engines and the crash and rescue stuff.

With all this in mind it would be of benefit to teach myself to drive so I availed myself of the opportunity and did a do it yourself job up and down the taxiways to such effect that I became the official jeep driver taking the FCOs backwards and forwards to the Wardroom and also driving myself and oppos. around the very large airfield.

RAF 45 Sqdn. Beaufighter

First flight of Air Ceylon

Other light relief came from the locals, always with an eye open for what could be 'liberated' and who could blame them bearing in mind their circumstances; thus a popular run was across the Bay from Kinnyah to see what could be won from the 24 end; this activity could be seen from the Tower and the drill was to leap into the Jeep, suitably armed with Very pistols and smoke puff cartridges, and belt off down the taxiway.

By the time we arrived they had taken fright and were paddling like mad in the outrigger canoes but not, as was discovered, out of range of the smoke puffs which landed alongside them and exploded with a loud bang and an impressive ball of reddish brown smoke whereupon the canoes almost became airborne in the attempts to get away; it was fortunate that no-one was harmed by this activity.

This was not the case with one unfortunate local tho' who had been removing telephone cable in the now deserted Natchykanda Camp and, unbeknown to him,the cables were holding the pole up, the bottom having been eaten away by termites and when the cable was cut the lot came crashing down killing him on the spot.

We were roaming around generally and became aware of the smell of a decomposing body and soon came across him, having been dead for some days and pretty much rotted and eaten away.

The Police were informed and a very drunk assistant did an autopsy there and then with what seemed to be a box of carpenters tools; all in all, a very forgettable procedure.

Whilst with Flying Control we had the only kit inspection since leaving training; well, with the war over something had to be found to keep the officers active and the Pusser regime was being re-introduced with a vengeance so all was laid out as per KR & AI and duly inspected by the Divisional Officer, Lt.Kenny.

The kit of a Jolly Jack Tar was considerable, an initial issue on joining up then upkeep by a small allowance included with pay and it all certainly cost the tax payer a great deal, but one item was completely superfluous and that was the tropical white duck suit which I never saw anyone wear and had to be kept clean and carried around, in all adding a lot to the tax bill and carriage costs for all 750,000 of us.

The normal tropical issue for RN was white cotton shorts with the standard cotton shirt, long navy blue socks and black shoes and, of course, a white top sailors cap; as FAA we wore tropical khaki which was not so difficult to keep clean.

Around this time was the Great Remuster, there being little demand for gunners and so forth as killings had declined somewhat so the troops were asked to volunteer for other branches, Writers, Cooks, Supply spring to mind. As I was deemed to have remustered myself to the FAA I took little interest in the proceedings.

By now instructions came down the line that many stores were to be disposed of by smashing them up or dumping as the airfield was to close, with the whole base following suit not long after, and so it proved to be.

I was the Duty Watch in the Tower and made the last calls without even the Duty Officer being in attendance.

"Trinco Tower, closing down, any last calls for Trinco Tower?"

All that came back was the usual hiss from the speaker; I made the appropriate entry in the log book, switched off all the equipment and left the Tower for the last time; no visiting Admirals, no brass bands, nothing; Trinco had passed into history.

Glider targets

TO/ GENERAL AT TRINCO. (R) R.N.O. COLOMBO.   FROM/ C IN C E I

CHRISTMAS 1946

XMAS DAY IS TO BE TREATED AS A GENERAL HOLIDAY AND SHIPS COMPANY'S
SHOULD FIRE DOWN IMMEDIATELY AFTER MORNING CHURCH.
2). THE C IN C'S OFFICE WILL NOT BE MANNED ON XMAS DAY BUT THE DUTY
STAFF OFFICER AND THE DUTY SECRETARY WILL BE AVAILABLE ON THE TELEPHONE.
3) THE FLEET MAIL OFFICE WILL BE OPEN UNTIL 1100 FOR A DISTRIBUTION
OF MAILS. THERE WILL BE NO DESPATCH ON XMAS DAY.
4). NORMAL ROUTINE IS TO BE WORKED ON XMAS EVE AND BOXING DAY.
5) THE DOCKYARD WILL BE CLOSED ON XMAS DAY EXCEPT FOR ESSENTIAL
SERVICES. XMAS EVE AND BOXING WILL BE NORMAL WORKING DAY.
CAPTAIN SUPT TRINCO HAS ISSUED DETAILED ORDERS.
6) R.N.O. IS TO PROMULGATE IN COLOMBO AREA.

                        D.T.G. 221002 DECEMBER.
P/H P/L   T.O.R. 221150.
TYPED MORRIS CHECKED REZIN.
DIST:- FULL STAFF AND STATION......................

NAVAL CANTEEN SERVICE, H.M.S. "BAMBARA."

RATION CARD

NAME... ROBERT ===== W.E. 720143

RATING...... A/B... OFFICIAL No.... c/8x

BEER	CIGARETTES
2 24/12/46	
25	90. 28/84

ATTACH THIS TO A BLANK PAGE OF YOUR PAY BOOK.

This form is an official Document and must Remain with the
owner until Going on draft when it is to be handed to the
records office.

P.T.O

HMS Uva/Diyalatawa Leave Camp

L eave in the RN was subject to conditions at the time, if you were in the UK there were no real problems but abroad it was quite impossible apart from compassionate reasons and even then it might take weeks to get home.

Faced with this problem leave camps were arranged, sometimes multi-service such that one could, for a time, escape the worst rigours of service life. One such was at Diyatalawa, previously a multi-service camp but now taken over by the RN as HMS Uva and situated in the central mountains about thirty five miles south east of the capital, Kandy, and, as Ike Elkins and myself considered that we were due for a spot of leave, we applied in the manner required by King's Regulations and Admiralty Instructions and this was duly approved.

Suitably kitted out in the civvy clothes run up by one of the camp tailors we mustered by the Guard Room and duly boarded the RN lorry that was to take us to the camp.

The first part of the journey was along the narrow roads, mainly through the jungle and meeting little in the way of traffic other than the usual bullock carts that were the standard transport; then we started to climb the foothills which got steeper as we got closer to the central mountains; the driver was a local who obviously knew the route like the back of his hand; progress was flat-out and this included round the sharp bends and up and down the hills; the roads were very narrow and there was no protection against the sheer drops just inches away.

This led to near panic so far as the Jolly Jack Tars were concerned, all clinging on for dear life as the lorry rocketed from one crisis to the next with the Petty Officer in charge constantly shouting at the driver to keep his eyes on the

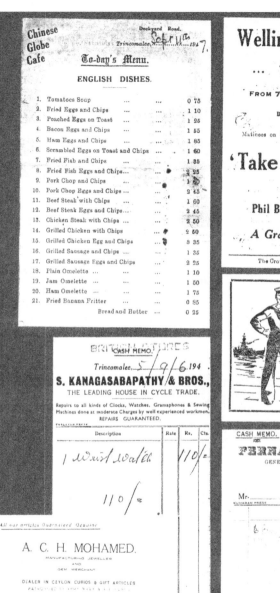

Chinese Globe Cafe

Dockyard Road.
Trincomalee, Feb 11th 194 7.

To-day's Menu.

ENGLISH DISHES.

1. Tomatoes Soup	... ...	0 75
2. Fried Eggs and Chips	... ...	1 10
3. Poached Eggs on Toast	... ...	1 25
4. Bacon Eggs and Chips	... ...	1 55
5. Ham Eggs and Chips	... ...	1 85
6. Scrambled Eggs on Toast and Chips	...	1 60
7. Fried Fish and Chips	... ...	1 35
8. Fried Fish Eggs and Chips	... ...	2 25
9. Pork Chop and Chips	... ...	1 80
10. Pork Chop Eggs and Chips	...	2 45
11. Beef Steak with Chips	...	1 60
12. Beef Steak Eggs and Chips	...	2 45
13. Chicken Steak with Chips	...	2 50
14. Grilled Chicken with Chips	...	2 50
15. Grilled Chicken Egg and Chips	...	3 35
16. Grilled Sausage and Chips	...	1 35
17. Grilled Sausage Eggs and Chips	...	2 25
18. Plain Omelette	... ...	1 10
19. Jam Omelette	... ...	1 50
20. Ham Omelette	... ...	1 75
21. Fried Banana Fritter	...	0 85
Bread and Butter	...	0 25

CASH MEMO.

Trincomalee, 5 / 9 / 6 194 .

S. KANAGASABAPATHY & BROS.,

THE LEADING HOUSE IN CYCLE TRADE.

Repairs to all kinds of Clocks, Watches, Gramaphones & Sewing Machines done at moderate Charges by well experienced workmen.
REPAIRS GUARANTEED.

Description	Rate	Rs.	Cts.
1 Wrist Watch		110/=	
		110/=	

All our articles Guaranteed Genuine

A. C. H. MOHAMED.

MANUFACTURING JEWELLER
AND
GEM MERCHANT

DEALER IN CEYLON CURIOS & GIFT ARTICLES
PATRONISED BY ARMY NAVY & AIR FORCE

DOCK YARD ROAD TRINCOMALEE,
Ceylon.

3394

CASH MEMO.

FERNANDO & RAYER,

GENERAL MERCHANTS & AGENTS.

Dockyard Road.

Trincomalee, 2 2 . 4 . 194 7

Mr.

KUMARAN PRESS

DESCRIPTION	Rate	Rs.	Ct.

432

Goods once sold will not be taken back

road, that worthy having an unhappy knack to turning round to talk to those behind him, quite oblivious of the potential ahead.

Despite all that the party arrived safely at Ramboda for a stop-off and we took the opportunity to see the famous waterfalls there and then visited the local guest house for a bite to eat, at the same time photographing the keeper's family, the prints of which I forwarded forty two years later though I never heard if they were received.

The journey continued through Nuwura Elyia and this proved to be most interesting in that here was an English town transported to Ceylon complete with half timbered houses, race course and tree lined streets.

It was the classic situation whereby the British colonists established residences in the most climatically favourable spots away from the intense heat of the coastal regions.

Next stop was the Camp, set in a bowl in the mountains and surrounded by really beautiful countryside, ideal for walks and general relaxation and I suppose we were there for a week and, for the first time in Ceylon, blankets were required at night time.

In the mornings there was no 'wakey,wakey' bugle, just a call by one of the catering staff with a cup of tea, and all day long we roamed around the local area visiting Buddhist temples and the like.

On a medical note, and for reasons quite unexplained, I managed to get utterly constipated, to be resolved by the dreaded No.9s which would have moved the Boulder Dam.

This was the area of the tea plantations, Ceylon at the time supplying a considerable proportion of the world's tea so we bought a few cases of Golden Orange Pekoe to send home to tea starved Britain.

The short leave away from the shouting and bull was most appreciated and enjoyed so back to Bambara.

Headquarters

Affter the airfield closed we became Ship's Company proper; gone was the relaxed atmosphere of Flying Control with the small staff and close relationship with the officer, gone the Special Duty status, khaki uniforms, few night watches; back to the usual shouting and bellowing from the senior rates who really thought there was no other way of handling people (perhaps there wasn't).

About this time there was a Pusser's issue of a completely new working rig, clearly copied from the US Navy and very sensibly too.

Normal working rig was Number Two, *ie*;for us chaps dressed as sailors, it was blue serge uniform worn without blue jean collar and sporting red badges and for the more dirty jobs, Number Three was worn, a set of blue cotton overalls; all these were replaced by a fairly heavy duty cotton shirt in medium blue and a pair of navy blue cotton jeans, the lot topped off with a navy beret which replaced the sailors' white topped cap.

In later times the cotton rig was replaced with a cotton and nylon mixture which wore better and melted on the wearer in the case of fire with quite disastrous results; no marks for that little lot.

Being available for general duties meant that I was, from time to time, obliged to do duty as Ceremonial Guard for visiting top brass and VIPs and this led to the usual clouds of Blanco and much arms drill, not much fun on the acres of concrete which heated up considerably.

I cannot recall if there was a Marine Band, most places did have one and, even now, if I hear *Hearts of Oak* or *A Life on the Ocean Wave* I want to stand to attention ready to march off for Divisions or whatever.

Certainly there was a bugler, one Nobby Clark from our Mess being renowned for his ultra clean attitude, to the extent of even polishing the soles of his Wellingtons.

Normal watchkeeping as sentry no longer escaped me as many guards were required all around the base; clothing stores, galley, main and small gates and so forth armed with a battered rifle and bayonet.

Night watches were quite pleasant, it was nice and warm and quiet and the only thing to disturb things was a visit from the Gunnery Officer, one Lt. Baker, who would roar up in his Jeep at unexpected moments accompanied by the duty RPO

"Halt,who goes there ?"and all that sort of stuff.

A notice appeared on the board one day asking for volunteers for a gunnery course so I put my name down and was eventually whisked off to the range somewhere north of Trinco.

Here we were to do a short course on the 20 mm Oerlikon, so following the usual preamble, rockets projected targets that slowly descended by parachute whilst we blazed away with HE, AP and Tracer.

In lighter moments, it was said, when an outrigger canoe paddled by the drill was to fire in the sea well in front of these unfortunates causing the projectiles to ricochet over the

JBL at Natchykanda Camp

paddlers, much to their consternation; all in all outriggers seemed to have had a hard time at the hands of the RN and they were probably pleased to see us depart.

This cannot have been the case generally, despite the stance of the Ceylon Nationalists with their 'Brits Out' all over the walls as the RN clearly contributed vast sums of cash locally in wages, purchases, rents *et al* and it must have been badly missed when Bambara finally closed and the British services withdrew from Ceylon.

It must have been about this time I was drafted, on a daily basis,to work aboard HMS Dabchick.

HMS Redshank

HMS Dabchick

Originally laid down at Beverley, Yorkshire with the intention of being an Isles Class trawler called *Thorney* she was modified to become an RN Bird Class Controlled Minelayer of 560 tons named *Dabchick* together with sister ships *Blackbird* and *Whitethroat*, additionally *Corncrake* and *Redshank* were converted from the slightly larger Fish Class trawlers.

Controlled minelayers were specially constructed for mining harbours and similar associated activities; defensively mined harbours generally took the form of a string of sea type mines linked by heavy electrical cables and sunk to the required place on the bed of a harbour, river or as appropriate and our job was to remove the mines across Trinco harbour mouth but there must have been others elsewhere as well as Redshank was there too.

Dabchick was tying up each night at HMS Highflyer and each day we puttered over there in one of the many launches that provided transport around the vast harbour and boarded for a day's work.

Close by was the beached wreck of SS Sagaing, bombed and run ashore during the April raids and full of burnt out tanks and lorries; I believe she is still there; also there was the rusting remains of AFD 26,having broken her back with HMS Valiant aboard and sunk by depth charges before the battleship went the same way; after many heroic failures and firms going bust, she was finally raised many years after the war.

Fishing up the mines was done by trawling a grappling hook in the hope of catching the mine cables and, when caught, reeled in via the large pulley built into the focsle and a steam driven winch on the deck amid much clanking and steam; the cable was covered in barnacles and made handling it dangerous work, also from time to time a mine would appear equally covered with barnacles and

HMS Dabchick

sea growth and looking very sinister indeed as they were filled with a large charge of explosive; the drill was to lift them via a small crane on the stern while the mine experts rendered them safe.

CPO Snell bashing out the detonator

This took the form of CPO Snell bashing out the detonator with a large hammer and chisel, an alarming practice accompanied by a general move towards the bows by those among us not familiar with this un-nerving procedure tho', had one exploded, it would have scattered Dabchick and her intrepid crew over a large part of Ceylon.

Once a few mines and the heavy cable had been collected we puttered out of the harbour and dropped the lot into deep water.

Dabchick was commanded by Lt.Cdr. P.E. Martin R.N.R.and was a 'Smokey Joe' that is to say a coal burner, one of only three such RN ships remaining in the Far East so it was said and conditions in the engine room must have been pretty frightful as it was extremely hot on deck and the stokers looked very pallid indeed when emerging for a breather.

By the time we returned to Bambara all the mines had been dealt with and Dabchick and Redshank continued round the Island to clear Colombo harbour. In 1954 she was sold off to the Malay Navy and became *Penu*; they sold her on again in 1959 and she may still be around; if so, "Here's to you Smokey Joe" forty five years on.

"Is it Safe?"
JBL peering round the mine.

Life at HQ.

Accommodation at HQ was decidedly in the luxury class so far as the RN was concerned being the beneficiary of the RAF station from the Great Days of Empire and almost all the buildings were well designed brick built structures indicating the permanent nature of the establishment.

As would be expected, the Wardroom stood on the top of a small hill behind the airfield so that it could catch the breezes; next down the hill was the Petty Officers mess and at the bottom,where there were no breezes worthy of mention lived the ratings,the Lower Deck to use a term from the Wooden Walls;A Block housed the FAA personnel and B Block Ships Company.

Additionally there was an armoury, parachute packing room, sick bay, Captains and Commanders offices and administration block, cinema, canteen, photographic section, met. office, more modest huts for the locals, large numbers of whom were employed around the airfield and so on; Five Mess, where I was installed had electric fans always revolving, sprung metal frame beds, mosquito nets and a small wardrobe for each man, the bedding being supplied by ourselves in the form of the hammocks we carried, part of this consisting of a Kapok filled mattress which required frequent 'picking' to keep it comfortable, tho' it must be bourne in mind that picking Kapok was also a punishment enjoyed by those in the cells.

After a time one of the small rooms became available with space for four beds thus a bit more private so I moved there with Ike Elkins, Hartnell and Kemp and was there until leaving Bambara.

Washing and Dhoby facilities were splendid tho' I cannot recall hot water ever being available, in any event the water supply was always luke warm and heavily dosed with chlorine and frequently restricted in supply.

C in C Inspection, JBL in there somewhere.

L/S Kemp

Most personnel got their dhobying done by the locals of whom there were a profusion on the airfield, the preferred method being to bash the dirty clothing against a smooth stone, some had specially shaped concrete blocks, and then left it dry in the hot sun then ironed; in any event the results were always sparkling white and very cheap.

Food always seemed to be adequate, cooked by the locals; bangers (soya link sausages) and red lead (tinned tomatoes) was a very popular item and they managed, as always, to serve up a splendid Christmas dinner for 1946, served by the Officers as tradition demanded.

At the doorway to the mess hall stood a large vat of lime juice into which everyone dipped their cups thus spreading around what might have been on them; it must have been worth it as there were no known cases of scurvy. From what I recall, Christmas 1946 was the event of the Very Pistol Affair whereby we of Ship's Company were relaxing in the mess when a Very Light came whistling over from the direction of the FAA block and spluttered around the mess emitting much smoke and sparks.

Not to be outdone by this intrusion and, as Flying Control, had the keys to the pyrotechnic stores, we promptly armed ourselves appropriately and proceeded to battle it out with the FAA via variously coloured lights and smoke puffs.

Xmas 1946

The air became quite thick with arching Very Lights and it was inevitable that someone in authority would see it all, Christmas or no Christmas, and, of course they did; the duty Crushers were soon on the scene with the duty Officer and trouble was on the way.

It was fortunate no-one was injured by this excess and no damage done though of course this might not have been the case and the whole camp could have been razed to the ground.

The case was too serious for Divisional Officers Report so we were referred to Commander's Report which was a pretty serious situation with quite severe penalties to be expected.

One of my fellow miscreants was Kemp whose mother was knee deep in Scientology and to whom he dispatched a vastly expensive cable explaining all and asking her to apply 'influence' on the Commander at the time of the Report; in effect cast a spell on him.

We were duly marched in, 'Off Caps, Able Seaman Lindop *et al*, did, contrary to King's Regulations & Admiralty Iinstructions etc. etc. What did we have to say?...what could we say except to admit that we idiots, with which the Commander heartily agreed and sentenced us to some trivial loss of leave, and, as we hardly ever went ashore, it was almost a non event and we didn't even have to pay for the Very Lights.

Naturally, Kemp was cock a hoop, claiming, with good reason, that the day had been saved by his mother's spell and who could argue with that ?

To add to the loss of shore leave I split a tooth on a date stone and was obliged to seek the services of the well equipped dental section where, after extracting the nerve, a small cap affixed with a steel post was fitted; alas, it constantly came out so was eventually discarded until about 1980 when a permanent solution was adopted.

Health matters in general were well attended to with a large sick bay and staff of Sick Bay Attendants (SBAs) and Doctors; serious cases could be referred to the Fleet Hospital at Highflyer.

One piece of light relief was the frequent

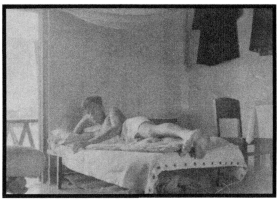

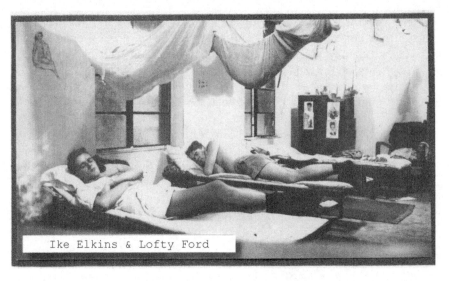

Ike Elkins & Lofty Ford

inoculations of the whole Ship's Company and this was effected by having several vast queues in the hangars with medical personnel at the head of each administering the jabs.

Naturally the floor was soon covered with the recumbent figures of those who had flaked out so someone thought of the ripping wheeze of hiding the jabbing positions and swoonings thereafter declined somewhat.

Pay parades, monthly, were also held in the main hangar with the Warrant Paymaster and his retinue in command; I no longer recall what we received in the large, florid Ceylon notes and oddly shaped coins except that it was helped along by tropical pay, Japanese Campaign money and, it was said, a small donation from the Ceylon Government along with some cigarettes.

HMS Highflyer

Despite the poor pay money was never a real problem as there was nowhere to go to spend it apart from a monthly run ashore to Trincomalee and the odd trip to the canteen or Kate Kearney's.

Shopping at HQ was modest; apart from the canteen there were various establishments run by the locals selling all sorts of consumer items, some of which were not available at home, such as nylon stockings.

Additionally, there were tailors, hairdressers, shoemakers and so forth and it was discovered that one of the latter made excellent jack boots so there was an outbreak of that item in the mess after that.

Whether this flush of jackboots had anything to do with it I do not know but writings began to appear on the walls to the effect 'Brits Out' perhaps mirroring the

'Yanks Go Home' in the UK; also leaflets appeared quite obviously inspired by Communist thinking, appealing to us oppressed ratings to rise against our officers and join them in the Workers Utopia that lay just around the corner.

It all seemed a bit like *Mutiny on the Bounty* and, so far as I know, there was no large scale insurrection, nor one of any size for that matter although there were considerable Nationalist rumblings around the Island generally and sentries were armed with live ammo.

Subsequently, of course, Brits, did Get Out and the Communists got their Utopia of a sort but this did not mean Tamils and The Others getting on together, ultimately leading to a bloodbath of intolerance.

All the locals I came into contact with were very friendly; the head of the labourers was a chap called Ishmael who lived in Kinnyah where his father ran a tea stall; we met him on the one, illegal, trip we did there via motor boat across the Bay with PO Wells in command.

On the way back a violent storm appeared from nowhere, as they were wont to do, and we very nearly foundered, saved in the main by the boating skills of PO Wells; a bit of a frightener.

Ceylon had both weather and climate;there were two Monsoons, the North East from December to March and the South West from June to September so much of the year had a vast rainfall hence the lush jungle.

Humidity became appalling in the torrents of rain, clothing went damp and mouldy and cigarettes so damp they would not burn; getting wet was almost a pleasure as the rain was warm.

September 3rd. 1947 was my 21st. birthday, also that of Minnie Moorhouse by a remarkable co-incidence, so a joint celebration was held in the mess, much assisted by locally brewed onion beer, drawn from Pussers stores in a bucket and helped down by Arack, a sort of palm tree gin of notorious potency. Alcoholic drink was freely available in the RN unlike the US Navy where they had more sense; the RN tradition stemmed from the days of the Wooden Walls when water was undrinkable and was replaced with rum and beer.

Rum was issued to all ratings up to CPO, I do not know if Warrant Officers were included in this but Officers had spirits available in their mess. Personnel were T, G or UA, that is to say, Temperence, Grog or Under Age; UA had an issue of lime juice in lieu and Temp. received 3d a day.

Grog was a watered down issue,two and one but if in a position of privilege such as watch-keepers etc. one could draw it 'neaters' and hoard it for a binge at a later date; it was 100 proof plus and certainly made ones eyes water and was also an accepted sort of Lower Deck currency, sippers for small jobs, gulpers for large ones and a whole tot for major events.

Many of the regulars, 'three badgers', were well hooked on the stuff and well on the way to being alcoholics; rum seemed to be at the root of many of the rackets in the RN, of which there were a profusion, and scrapping the issue probably did the service a good turn.

Life at Bambara was not all work and birthday parties; watch-keeping duties produced considerable spare time and this could be spent in a variety of ways depending on ones interests.

At HQ there was a large cinema showing all the popular films via the RN Film Unit; there was a Music Society whereby classical music was dispensed by the means of a wind up 78 rpm gramophone; dancing classes were held minus females and from time to time a concert party arrived, usually ENSA tho' Bambara put its own show on once whereby Ship's Company talent could display itself for better or worse, mostly the latter.

Being interested in radio I applied for a City & Guilds Forces course in Telecommunications Engineering and did quite a lot of it tho' I let it lapse after leaving Bambara.

I became friendly with several of the radio mechanics and spent a lot of time fiddling around in the radio workshops; Topsy Turner, a PO on the aircraft side ran an amateur radio set up on the then popular 7 and 14 mcs. and with that set we spoke to many around the world.

VS7IT was a rare callsign and there was much jostling to get a contact; there was quite a good library and a regular supply of daily papers tho' no doubt much out of date by the time they arrived.

Purchasing an 'export only' Kodak camera in Trinco I started to take an interest in photography and spent a lot of time rambling around the airfield snapping odds and ends to have them developed and printed in Trinco to quite a high standard.

Runs ashore, apart from the single leave to Diyatalawa, were always to

JBL and Cross

Trincomalee via the boat service, I cannot remember going anywhere else and, in any event, Trinco was the only town of any size for some considerable distance, all the other places being small villages with the attendant risks and best avoided anyway.

Trinco itself was not much more than a large village

with an array of shops where most of the usual things could be purchased.

We always went to the same cafe for grub, The Chinese Globe in the main street run by the inevitable Chinaman; I wonder if it is still there.

On one occasion we attended the Wellington Talkies in Trinco and sat through what must have been a years supply of Flash Gordon serial films, surely some sort of record.

Swimming was also popular at the Nicholas Road beach in Trinco, the water being so warm you were not really aware of being in it apart from the small stinging jellyfish.

On the odd occasion we went to the Fleet Canteen at Highflyer, now rebuilt after the Aussies had burnt it to the ground tho' there was little there that was different to the canteen at Bambara other than Black Horse beer available on production of a coupon of which we received one a month.

Tambalagam Bay

Cigarettes seemed to be available in unlimited quantities, unlike the UK where they were scarce indeed;a half pound tin of tobacco could be purchased for 2/6 (£.0.12) in the clothing stores and you rolled your own, known as 'ticklers', plus a monthly issue of fifty Players in a tin, free from the Ceylon Government, or so it was said.

Pets were a part of the hobby and interest scene; there was the odd monkey but they were regarded with disfavour not being too particular who they bit and were noisy and smelly as well; inevitably there were many dogs until rabies reared its ugly head close to the establishment so the order went out that they were all to be shot.

Sometime during my stay at Bambara a Demob number was allocated; there were three release schemes, A,B and C based on length of service, compassionate grounds, industrial requirements and so forth.

My number was 63 in the A scheme as I had no validity for accelerated release but for some reason the number was a long time in arriving and higher numbers than mine were appearing on the 'draft for home' board; I was starting to get the feeling that I had been forgotten when a list of names appeared on the Notice Board for a UK draft.

It was for 22nd. November 1947 and to be outside the Guardroom at 08:15 hours with all my kit; time in the RN was running out.

Amateur Radio VS71T

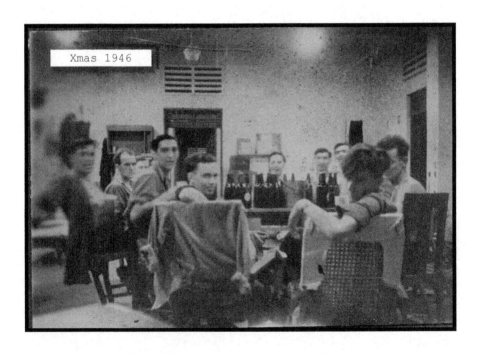

Xmas 1946

Part 3

After Bambara

The under-mentioned ratings report

at the car park outside The Guard Room

at 08:15 Saturday 22nd November

NAMES OF RATINGS AVAILABLE FOR PASSAGE TO THE UNITED KINGDOM IN H.M.T.

EMPRESS OF SCOTLAND.

RATINGS DUE FOR DISPOSAL BY 14th JANUARY 1948.

NAME.	RATING.	OFFICIAL NO.	A. & S. GR.	D.L.U.K.
BECKWORTH J.	A.B.	P/JX 783876	71	12th June, 46
LINDOP J.B.	A.B.	D/JX 540875	63	3rd Jan, 46
DUNCAN J.B.	A.B.	C/JX 642989	70	17th July, 46
WHALE P.B.	A.B.	C/JX 658123	63	28th Jan, 46
JAMISON L.	A.B.	C/JX 762257	69	13th July, 47
WARD J.	P.R.M.(W/T)	C/MX 705978	67	6th Nov, 46
BUCKINGHAM B.	TEL.	D/JX 714772	70	5th May, 47
DAVIES. J.M.J.	O/SIG.	D/JX 806156	75	5th May, 47.
HUSSEY. F.J.	O/TEL	D/JX 796201	73	3rd APRIL,47.
KILBURN. W.	O/TEL.	D/JX 796282	73	3rd APRIL,47.
JOHNSON. W.A.	O/TEL	D/JX 796862	74	5th MAY 47.
GEORGE.A.L.	E.R.A.4.	P/MX 802320	75	19th JAN. 47.
GARRY. I.G.	STO: MECH:	P/KX 775708	70	21st APL. 46.
WILSON. N.C.	STO:MECH:	P/KX 762442	69	25th FEB. 46.
WHITEHURST.G.	STO: MECH:	D/KX 761464	69	14th MCH. 46.
HIRONS. V.S.	STO: MECH:	D/KX 764369	69	14th MCH. 46.
CARTWRIGHT.J.	SHIPT.5.	D/MX 745241	75	17th JLY. 46.
CRIPPS. W.E.	SHIPT.5.	P/MX 716977	74	3rd DEC. 46.
CURRAN. J.B.	A.A.(H)	FX 716109	69	18th FEB 47.
RIACH.W.D.	A.A.(MW)	FX 768263	70	1st NOV 46.
HARTNELL. D.J.	A.B.(AH)	P/JX 706767	70	6th NOV 46.
HILL.M.J.	A.B.(AH)	P/JX 773708	70	6th NOV 46.
HILL.J.W.	A.B.(AH)	P/JX 773366	70	6th NOV 46.

RATINGS WHO WILL HAVE COMPLETED TWO YEARS FOREIGN SERVICE BY 15th DECEMBER, 1947.

SUMMERS.R.J.	A.A.(O)	FX 82538	C.S.	19th JLY. 45.
McKAY. J.	A.A.	D/JX 151788	C.S.	15th NOV. 45.
WEATHERBURN.F.	A.A.	D/JX 155445	C.S.	22nd NOV. 45.
NUTTAL. J.N.S.	A.A.	P/JX 581355	C.S.	22nd NOV. 45.
HEATHER.I.	A.A.	P/JX 712202	C.S.	24th NOV. 45.
KEMP. J.R.	A.A.SIG.	P/JX 581944	C.S.	5th DEC. 45.
COOK. L.R.	A.B.	P/JX 581481	C.S.	5th DEC. 45.
BASHER. P.D.	A.B.(O)	P/JX 581300	C.S.	5th DEC. 45.
CRIPPS. F.	A.B.(AH)	P/JX 427707	C.S.	14th DEC. 45.

HMT Empress of Scotland

Being a Rating for Passage to the UK I duly presented myself at the car park by the Guard Room at the appointed time and heaved my kit and baggage aboard the lorry that was to take us to the station, retracing the journey of nearly two years ago.

As usual it was going to be another hot day as I looked around at the familiar surroundings; the airfield now closed, the Control Tower also closed and empty; Malay Cove Camp across the road, also closed and deserted; the Wardroom, Petty Officers Mess and ratings barrack blocks, they all looked very permanent and busy with hurrying figures, this had been my home for two years and now I was leaving it for good, probably never to see it again.

No more red lead and soya link sausages, no more guards for visiting brass hats, no more trips into Trinco for big eats and iced coffee.

I cannot recall being sorry to leave all this, the only thought was to get home again for by now, with my Demob. number well up, a feeling was starting to emerge that I had been forgotten and likely to live out my days forever marooned at Trinco, never to see my family and friends again.

There were thirty three of us on the draft, most of them I knew quite well though now many details have faded; Kemp from my mess, elevated to Leading Seaman; the Hill twins and Hartnell are all I can now recall.

I suppose we boarded the train at China Bay Halt and traveled across the Island to Columbo but I recall nothing of the journey.

H.M.Transport *Empress of Scotland* was anchored in the harbour at Columbo so we had to reach her via a ferry, there was a gangplank at some impossible angle and, loaded up with kitbag, hammock, suitcase etc. there was a point where I thought I would not make it but was hauled safely aboard by a helpful subby. and deposited in a small ten bunk cabin simmering at some one

HMT Empress of Scotland, Malta

HMT Empress of Scotland, Liverpool

hundred and fifty degrees, no scuttle and precious little ventilation; ideal for the colder weather as we got closer to home, or so the Petty Officer assured us. This lasted about a half hour then we were evicted for some officers and relegated to the hold with the masses.

Empress of Scotland started life as *Empress of Japan* but did a rapid change of name when Japan entered the war on the wrong side; she displaced some 26,032 tons when built by Fairfields in 1929 for the Canadian Pacific Steamship Co. in the great days of the ocean liners, having a crew of five hundred and eighty to service twelve hundred passengers.

As a trooper she carried some four thousand two hundred and was quite definitely cramped to say the least and, judging by the red duster flag, she was crewed by Merchant Navy personnel.

According to my Service Certificate we sailed for home on November 27th., the first stop being Aden to pick other hopefuls for UK and demob. but there was no shore leave; next stop was Malta after traversing the Suez Canal, thence to Gibraltar and then Liverpool on a cold wet grey day;there was even a band playing for us; it was December 24th. 1947 and we disembarked on to an equally cold wet and grey quayside and entrained for Guzz.

Few memories have survived concerning the passage home which must have taken about a month; there was nothing to do other than loaf about with the other four thousand odd assorted servicemen and the high spots of the day were meal times with recreation mainly watching the world go by, which, being mostly water, was not exactly taxing on the intellect.

Consolation took the form of consideration of how much it would have cost us had we been passengers with the Canadian Pacific Steamship Company.

Empress of Scotland's last trooping trip ended at Liverpool on May 8th. 1948 when she was finally demobbed, went for refit and returned to her old job as a cruise liner this time for seven hundred passengers but no steerage, times they were a'changing.

On September 7th. 1966 she caught fire whilst in New York and was so badly damaged that she was scrapped at Hamburg; she too had lasted thirty seven years.

Demobilisation

M y Service Certificate notes my being at RNB Devonport from December 24th.1947 but it is not clear if we were in transit thus Christmas on the railways or actually in the Barracks.

I have no recollections whatsoever of Christmas that year, all I do know was that, after completion of joining routine, we all went on leave, the first for two years so it was probably fourteen days.

Returning to RNB I bumped into various old class mates from training days at Royal Arthur and Glendower and they told me that Joe Lewis, Red Rae, Taylor and various close friends had passed thro' Guzz only a few weeks before on the way to Demob; alas, I had missed them.

At RNB was something called 'The Whereabouts Office', official function unclear, so I availed myself of their services and obtained a few addresses for future use; forty years on I was to attempt to contact them but, apart from one instance, there was no response.

I was to remain at RNB for about three months occupied by the inevitable working parties one of which was the assist in the erection of a Bailey Bridge on the Hoe for some military exhibition and, on another occasion,to help move the Plymouth Sea Cadets to a new HQ.

Some time before March 16th. Demob Routine was commenced; the Demob Centre was St. Budeaux Camp so I suppose I spent a few days there doing the rounds whereby all the final paperwork was attended to and civvy clothes issued. To enter civilian life again there was the considerable paraphernalia of the Austerity State; identity cards, clothing coupons, food coupons for almost

Father, Thelma, Mother, Barbara

everything, postwar gratuities, pay slips, in fact a very considerable pile of paperwork all in a large envelope.

Most of our RN kit had to be handed in apart from what we were actually wearing, usually Number Ones which we owned anyway plus a few odds and ends like shoe brushes and Pussers issue knife which I still have.

The issue of civvy clothes was quite comprehensive consisting of a suit or equivalent, mac, hat, underwear, socks, shoes etc. and was of quite reasonably quality and, in fact, lasted quite a long time.

Having completed the routine and collected all the necessary documentation and civvy clothes it was all too suddenly time to say goodbye to the RN.

The Newsreels frequently showed the odd Admiral shaking hands with a demobbed Matloe and thanking him for his service to the RN but I no longer recall if anyone did that for me, if so it certainly was not an Admiral, perhaps a warrant officer or maybe a lieutenant, perhaps no-one at all.

Suddenly I was outside the door, still in my RN uniform, but no longer in the Royal Navy.

Even at this distance in time it is hard to put into words what my emotions were at this moment; for years I had looked forward to the event but now it was actually here there was a severe anti-climax.

Only moments before I had been a proud member of the RN with a guarantee of food, wages, accommodation, clothing, a career, general security and a measure of excitement too; now, in those few brief seconds a vast, almost uncrossable gulf had opened between me and them and, although I was dressed in the uniform of a Matloe it was really a sham and I was, in reality, a civvy masquerading in a sailor's suit and that great privilege of being in the RN had gone for ever.

Standing alone in the street I suddenly felt a great sadness and very much lost; a strange longing came over me to get back through that door again to meet

Westbury, Queen's Park, Chester

my old oppos with whom I had enjoyed great comradeship, excitement and danger.

Now it was gone for ever, I gritted my teeth and walked down the road to catch a bus to Plymouth and a train home.

There I met others similarly demobbed; I presented my final Travel Warrant and boarded the train for Chester.

Inevitably we had to change at dear old Crewe station; many a time in years past I had waited for hours on its bleak wind swept platforms but this time it was different, I was on the way home.

Waiting for the connection we went for a drink and, rushing for the train, tripped over my non regulation bell bottoms, always a hazard and quite unbeknowingly dropped the envelope containing all my Demob papers.

Finally arriving home after endless stops on the worn out railways I discovered this loss and took myself off to the Police Station to register the catastrophe which was of major proportions as it was impossible to do anything without the mass of paperwork, not the least be fed without the food coupons.

Happily the problem was resolved within a week as someone had picked up the envelope at Crewe and handed it in to the Police and it found its way back via the local Police in Chester.

I was immensely grateful to this unknown saviour as it saved a very great amount of trouble in obtaining new papers and was doubly grateful as coupons of this sort were worth quite a lot of money on the black market. I was now an ex-Matloe, all that had to be done was to pack away my uniform, apply for my medal and look around for a career of which I had not the slightest clue.

I had been in the RN three years and seven months, four years since first volunteering as a Youth Entry; I was an expert on various types of Search and Warning Radar, a good shot with a 20 mm Oerlikon cannon, excellent on gunnery, torpedoes and RN life in general but I had an uneasy feeling that there was not a lot of call for attributes of that sort in civvy life.

The door was closing slowly on that aspect of history that had been Able Seaman J.B.Lindop, RP3, D/JX 540875; it was the end of the road.

The Publisher Says:

Sometime after leaving the Navy, John met, fell in love and married Dorothy Davies. Together they have researched the Davies family tree and published their work in:

Davies of the Clwyd Valley
by John Barford Lindop
and Dorothy Lindop nee Davies

Published by Mercianotes
ISBN 9781905999231

Postscript

If a vacuum can descend it certainly did on me, here I was, home at last with no idea as to what was to happen to me so far as a career was concerned, I was now twenty two and several vital years had been lost in service to the country; I had never had a job except in the RN and, as previously suspected, there did not seem to be a lot of civilian demand for radar operators or dead shots with an Oerlikon, other avenues would have to be explored.

One of these was a Radio Operator in the Merchant Navy so a letter was sent off to the Marconi School in Liverpool for a prospectus; I do not recall now why the idea was finally rejected, perhaps I had been away long enough and certainly the market was excessively flooded with ex-service radio personnel, but rejected it was and, for a time, I wandered around Chester, probably for the fifty six days demob leave, garbed in bits and pieces of RN clothing and very much a fish out of water.

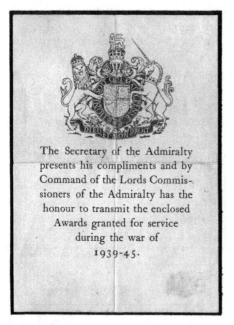

The Secretary of the Admiralty presents his compliments and by Command of the Lords Commissioners of the Admiralty has the honour to transmit the enclosed Awards granted for service during the war of 1939-45.

There was no petrol for motoring, and not much else either as everything of consequence was on ration and the buzz word was 'Austerity',which it most certainly was.

With an eye on entering the family firm of drapers I applied for a Forces Resettlement Course in Business Administration and duly presented myself for appraisal before a panel of worthies somewhere in Liverpool.

Closely questioned by said worthies I flopped the interview so tried again; the same thing happened as they were of the opinion that I would get no-where in Business Administration and thus no course.

It is ironic, in retrospect, that Business Administration was the one feature at which I excelled and most of my commercial life has been that of manager/company secretary/business organiser and related activities.

Well, it doesn't matter now and I suppose the worthies are long dead but one might be excused for wondering what qualifications they had for their job and what ability for spotting talents; it may well be as a consequence of their inabilities many went on to be square pegs in round holes and a lifetime of job misery.

A few months after Demob. a pay warrant arrived and a note telling me that this was for being in Class A Reserve which was now canceled; this came as a complete surprise as no-one had mentioned any reserves either in the RN or at Demob.; one can now speculate that recall was possible, indeed, likely tho' who we would then be fighting was a mystery.

Now we know it would have been the Russians as, we are frequently told, Stalin had designs on the whole of Europe tho' there seems little or no evidence in favour of this theory except that it supported the worst excesses of anti-Communist propaganda at the time, mainly American, even to the extent of keeping some of the Wehrmacht fully armed just in case, a really splendid piece of irony.

As time went by pieces of uniform wore out or were replaced by civvy clothes, the tin of 'tickler' tobacco was running out when Sir Stafford Cripps announced his extra super Austerity Budget increasing taxes in all directions and, in particular, that on tobacco so it seemed a good time to give up smoking which I promptly did thereby saving a good deal of cash and removing, largely, the possibility of smoking related illness.

The employment situation was resolved, for a time, in that a position was found for me at Thomas Woods, Electrical Engineers in Chester; they specialised in motor rewinds, light switchgear and so forth so it was home from home after RN radar.

Two years in the Tropics then started to tell and the very hard winter proved to be difficult in the extreme although you do not realise just how bad things are until they are retrospective.

This excursion into electrical engineering did not last long and plans were laid to join the family firm, however experience in that direction was much lacking so I took myself off to the John Lewis Partnership for a few years to learn the ropes in London, Liverpool and Chester where I found many ex-RN personnel beating swords into plough-shares.

By now it was the early fifties and we accompanied some friends to stay at Plymouth so took the opportunity to visit old haunts, tho' the centre of Plymouth had been rebuilt and was unrecognisable.

Guzz, from the safety of the car looked the same, the clock tower, the main gate with the PO of the Watch as in days past, perhaps the very chap who had been there when I passed thro' for the last time; time seemed to have stood still for a brief moment; then round to have a look at St. Budeaux Camp, still exactly the same but now housing Wrns so we were told, I hope conditions were better than in my day.

The following year we moved house and the year after we were married and the days of being a Jolly Jack Tar were fading rapidly into history as I applied myself to building a career and a family; RN photos and odd ephemera had been consigned to the attic and service in the RN was starting to look a bit like a dream.

Sometime later, in the early sixties I discovered the list of names and addresses mentioned earlier and wrote all around but apart from contacting Herbie Wiggins all the other letters came back 'Unknown'; Taylor, Commander Cartwright, Ike Elkins, Red Rae and all the others, are you there ?

By now the past was starting to catch up; whilst sweating away in the Control Tower at Trinco I had pledged myself that, fate being on my side, I would return one day with a Pilots Licence and do what the RN, in its wisdom, had decreed I was not suited to do, that is to say fly an aircraft myself from Trinco., and be on the other side of the R/T.

Forty was just around the corner, if I did not learn at this point I never would so the plunge was taken and a Private Pilots Licence eventually obtained, so the plan was working - so far anyway.

The next part was to get to Ceylon, now Sri Lanka, and do the flight but various events conspired against this course of action until the 1980's when I started to write a few letters and got encouraging replies to the effect that I would be permitted to fly one of the Cessna 150 aircraft of the Sri Lanka Defense Force from Trinco but before any action could be taken civil war exploded and still pertains today so any visit will have to wait until stability returns one day perhaps?

Around about that time we visited North Wales, in part to look for the long gone HMS Glendower and, in another guise, 95% of it it is still there to this day, clearly recognisable from the road and internally, little changed from the days when the RN was there tho' the trees have grown a bit and it is strangely in colour, unlike the old photos which is how I remember it.

Walking round the camp the place was filled with ghosts, it seemed such a short time ago we were all there so in a bout of maudlin nostalgia I wrote an article about it for a club magazine and the following is how I felt on that occasion.

HMS Glendower Revisited

Today, I said to my assembled family, we will try to find HMS Glendower and, as we were staying in Criccieth the journey would not be too long. The day was baking hot as we sped along the road and suddenly it looked familiar; Afon Wen Laundry the sign announced, had we not seen this sign when we passed it and repassed in that other life forty years ago on route marches, PT runs around the Camp or from the misted windows of the ship's 'launch' *enroute* for rowing and sailing in Pwllheli harbour.

Parking the car outside the Main Gate it looked much as when I had first seen it as we came from the Skegness Camp of HMS Royal Arthur, yet another Butlins, then by train in bleak unheated carriages carrying us goodness knows where but announced as HMS Glendower, somewhere in the wilds of Wales to be initiated into the mysteries of Seamanship, Gunnery, Radar, polishing mess tins with Bluebell and learning magic words like 'Aye Aye Sir', 'Pussers', 'Ashore', and 'Port and Starboard'.

At the side of the Main Gate the old Guard Room still stood, what memories it must hold in its stone walls; many a time I was on duty here as a 'runner of the day' carrying who knows what great secrets around the Camp.

Now the barbed wire was gone and the sentry strangely absent from his post. Passing by with my family I became aware that they should not be treading this hallowed ground,somehow they were intruding, trespassing on one of H.M. Ships and I was again a young Matloe; somehow the years had slipped away. In an attempt to find our old chalet I had, in my minds eye, a vision of Taylor, Red Rae or Joe Lewis laying out their kit for yet another inspection or perhaps preparing for a very rare shore leave but try as I might the chalet eluded me leaving me disappointed and confused.

What about the Gunnery section or perhaps the Wrns quarters with sentries and barbed wire around; as we walked in that direction I could see the old RN flooding by in their archaic uniforms, intent on the mission ahead but try as I might to touch them they dissolved to my gaze and I then knew that they were gone for ever from this place.

The walk down to the end of Pen y Chain Point was long and hot, the old assault course with its cliff immediately identifiable and the buildings of the small farm still in place; many a time when on guard duty we had called there for sandwiches from the kindly farmer, carrying on his occupation regardless of the mayhem all around; where is he now I wonder ?

From the end of the Point we had fired the 4" QF and been startled by the blast; the 0.5 Brownings and 20 mm Oerlikon with tracer, AP and explosive projectiles arching into the sky.

For reasons now forgotten we once slept in the ammo. Hut, or slept if we could as it was cruel on this windswept coast in the winter.

Below us was the beach of shingle were Joe and I gathered winkles for boiling in the galley by Wrn Cook Bunty and which beach we guarded at night in case of invasion carrying ancient Lee Enfield Mk. 1 rifles and five rounds of much dented ammunition to fend off the might of the Wehrmacht. We met the Coastguard halfway along the beach and gave the Password, 'Nelson" for what else could it be ?

Somewhere down there, on dark, cold stormy nights ghostly Matloes still meet the Coastguard, waiting for an invasion that will never now come; I know for I am one of them with legions of others who have trod the same path.

All that remained of our presence there were the rotting concrete platforms where the guns once stood, the rusting securing bolts gradually moldering away and the platform of the old ammo. hut quiet with their memories.

On the way back towards the Main Gate we passed the site of the old Parade Ground and I thought that I could hear, faintly on the wind, the shouts and orders of drilling Matloes.

Near by was the pit that held the Camps sole defense against aerial attack, a 20 mm Oerlikon; "Whats an Oerlikon, Daddy ?"

Many a time I had stood guard here waiting for the call but it never came; by the Main Gate was the swimming pool, then holding Whalers for rowing practice, now holiday makers sported in the welcoming waters and, nearby, was the saluting base where the Captain took the salute at morning Divisions and, as we marched by,our Instructors desperately searching for that special sign that was awarded for the excellence of our performance.

Across the road the Sick Bay once stood and where I was incarcerated with a vast temperature whilst the rest of the class went on 'End of Training' Leave with goodness knows what ahead.

The Jolly Campers now seemed obscene, where were the smart uniforms, the restless activity, the sense of purpose that had brought us together here all those years ago; I had an almost irresistible urge to rush up to them and tell them that here once stood His Majesty's ship Glendower, where part of that great multitude had trained for World War Two but had now slipped away into history. As we walked thro' the gate it became 1984 again and I was a father with a family and the past seemed hard to believe; was it really me who had been here all those years ago, it just does not seem credible.

As evening fell and the shadows lengthened I looked back at yesterday's memories and yes … in the darker corners I could now see shadowy figures in blue serge suits and bell bottom trousers, for they are there for all of us with eyes to see and, just below the surface of Butlins, HMS Glendower is lying, quietly slumbering, waiting for the call should Britain once again be threatened.

I suppose that it was about this time that the FAA Museum opened at Yeovilton and, being in the area a visit was demanded.

Apart from being dark and freezing cold as the electricity supply had failed it proved to be a most interesting if sobering experience.

Wt. 21115/D7753. 10,000 Pads. 9/46. B.B.LTD. 51-7213.

Form S. 1599   Created in HMS Bambara

DUPLICATE—To be sent to Officer or Rating.

WAR GRATUITY & POST WAR CREDIT of WAGES
to be deposited in the POST OFFICE SAVINGS BANK

P.O.S.B. ACCOUNT PARTICULARS

H.M.S. N.S

No. 455160

SURNAME (in block letters)	MR. MRS. MISS *LINDOP*
Full Christian Names	*John Harford*
Rank or Rating and Official No.	*A/AB D/JX540875*
Permanent Address (give full postal address) ..	
Date when amount is due to be deposited in the Savings Bank	*31st October 1946.*

	Service From	Service To	Unpaid Time Days	Net reckonable Service Months	Assessable Rank or Rating	Rate per month	Amount Payable £	s.	d.
War Gratuity	11 Sept. 44	15 Aug. 46	–	23	A/A/B.	10/-	11	10	–
			Days			per day			
Post War Credit of Wages in respect of Service as a Rating after 31-12-41.	11 Sept. 44	30 June 46	–	658	–	6 d	16	9	=
					–				

	£	s.	d.
Total amount of War Gratuity and Post War Credit	£	27	19	–
Less deduction in respect of outstanding charges on pay account, etc.	£	–	–	–
Amount for deposit	£	27	19	=

Date of dispersal to leave ....

Date of termination of Foreign Service Leave.....................................
(if any)

Date of release...   Date............

B Spence WWO
Signature and rank of Certifying Officer

1st December 46

Cut along this line

If you wish to change the address to which the Bank Book is to be sent, detach and post this slip to the Post Office Savings Bank, 25 Church Street, Manchester, 4.

You must insert here the number shown above. ☞

P.O.S.B. ACCOUNT PARTICULARS

H.M.S.............................

No.............................

SURNAME (in block capitals) ....

Christian Names (in full) ....

New Address.....................................

....

Is this address permanent ?.....................................

Date.............................   Signature of Officer or Rating

116

129

There, mounted and stuffed as prized antique exhibits were the very sorts of aircraft that had been the bread and butter of existence at RNAS Trinco during my stay there; no longer the gouts of flame, the whining starters, the bangs of Koffman cartridges, the slow clatter of beefy radials and the spluttering roar of Merlins.

Now all was silent and still, the Seafire, Walrus, Swordfish and others once throbbing and vibrant now looked down at me from the pages of history and I looked back at them, myself a part of their history forty seven years ago. Ten years flew by and the RN was an increasingly distant dream and may have been eliminated completely if it had not been for one momentous event. The British Museum had an exhibition of ancient Egyptian relics from the King Tutenkamen era and as the family were very interested we went to inspect it all and, at the same time, viewed the retired Town Class cruiser HMS Belfast moored at the Embankment and operated by the Imperial War Museum as a memorial to the war at sea during World War Two.

The effect of this visit was nothing short of electric, quite suddenly forty odd years were swept away and all the old RN memories came flooding back as a consequence of roaming round the messdecks and ship generally.

From what I could see she was almost identical to HMS Newcastle and I was immediately transported back in time, notwithstanding date and attendant family, to the period when I was on her and to say it was an eerie feeling was to understate the position; here I was walking round a ghost.

On the way around the ship I came across Navy News and was enthralled by the contents; the pattern forward was now clear, Able Seaman Lindop was to be reinstated, this would be the future research programme.

The moment was opportune as some ten years extensive efforts had gone into researching Lindop Family History, and having more or less completed that item, I was casting about for something to research next.

Just after this situation arose the family decided to visit the Isle of Man; it was retracing my steps of forty odd years before as we again went by sea though SS Snaefell had gone to the breakers many years before.

We looked for Valkyrie among the holiday makers, also the training school on Douglas Head; I wrote an article about it at the time and it is reproduced as follows.

Valkyrie - A Quest

Now almost forgotten, an overnight rail journey had brought us from the Seaman and Gunnery Training Camp of HMS Glendower in the wilds of Wales to a bleak quayside in the cold of an early morning.

'Fleetwood' someone had announced as we boarded *S.S.Snaefell* of the quaintly named Isle of Man Steam Packet Company, a twin funnelled ferry that was to take us to Douglas and *HMS Valkyrie* there for training in one of the great secrets of World War Two - radar no less and, at the end of training we would be fully fledged radar operators, RP3s in all the glory of Telegraphists wings with P beneath and expert in Air and Surface Search and Warning radars; types 271, 281, 277 and 291, 1000 Kw of RF burning the skies.

Suddenly I was on *SS Monas Isle* and it was forty years on, would Valkyrie be there to welcome me, were some of my old class mates perhaps waiting for another tram ride to Laxey, Joe Lewis, Red Rae, Taylor, those ghosts from the long past flickered before my eyes as we ploughed a wake towards Douglas now looming on the horizon, Snaefell reaching to the clouds beyond.

The years had scarcely changed Douglas harbour tho' the barbed wire was missing and no begaitered Petty Officer appeared from the crowds to fall us in and march us off.

In the background the sweep of Douglas Bay was lined with those same hotels that had welcomed us to Valkyrie, now their windows stared back at me with bland unseeing eyes;somewhere there Valkyrie was there waiting, waiting to see again one of her sons return and yes, dark against the sky the Douglas Head Hotel, its battlemented Victorian walls still there, grey and gloomy as before but the forest of science fiction aerials strangely missing.

Was Valkyrie gone for ever I wondered or was there perhaps some message left for me by all those who had worked and wondered all those years ago.

We were staying in my sister's comfortable home, vastly different from the barracks of Valkyrie; then holes had been knocked in the walls to join the hotels together to form the single unit that became Valkyrie, our home.

Little seemed to have changed and the ripple caused by the war had come and gone with no sign of its passing on these stone buildings.

Life now seemed quiet and peaceful; then all was rush and bustle and an overall sense of purpose pervaded all our being; at nights, and most of the days, the fog horn blew, its deep reverberating bellow shaking the whole town almost as tho' the old Celt and Norse gods were complaining of their beautiful island being defiled by war.

In the search for Valkyrie Loch Promenade looked familiar, now busy with holiday makers and many cars; then half its width formed our parade ground surrounded with barbed wire and sentries on the gates.

Now it was gone leaving no trace on the ground, no trace that once one of His Majesty's ships had stood here and, try as I might to identify it, one building looked like another and Valkyrie was keeping her secret.

I spoke to an hotel keeper, sunning himself where we had paraded; he had heard of Valkyrie, his hotel had been part of it, he still had blankets marked Valkyrie; suddenly the past reached from the shadows and touched me with ghostly fingers.

Leaving Loch Promenade to the ghosts we made our way to what had been the training school, passing on the way the fine Victorian cast iron clock, still keeping the time now as it had in that other life as we marched past in columns, lanterns at the head and rear for our training on the sets was at night due to the pressure of requirements for radar operators;past the harbour and up the endless steps leading to Douglas Head, all Admiralty property then and surrounded by barbed wire to keep out prying eyes for radar was the great secret; now the wire had gone and the road thronged with holiday makers with Manx Radio occupying the building erected by the RN to house the Search and Warning radar sets.

No sign of the marching columns, no sign of the strange aerials that had festooned every vantage point, types 271, 291, 281, 284, 285, 277, on the roof, on the ground, on a tower specially built.

Surely some sign left for me ?

I felt the pressure of the old RN everywhere for I feel sure that at nights, in the cold and wet, with the old fog horn bellowing, marching columns still form up outside the barracks, lanterns twinkling as in the time of long ago, to carry out their ghostly training.

Everywhere their shadows flitted by as we retraced our steps from yesterday's Valkyrie to today's Douglas and forty plus years on.

Valkyrie had, in a way, eluded us; somewhere in the long Manx history it is locked into the stone walls waiting to tell the tale to those who have the eyes to see and the ears to listen.

As we sailed away from Douglas harbour, repeating the journey of many years ago I looked back at Douglas Head and Loch Promenade for the vanished Valkyrie, but the buildings stared back expressionless and I knew then that they knew where Valkyrie was but it was locked in their stone hearts and they were keeping it.

In the furtherance of research various ex Naval organisations were joined and many adverts. placed in the technical press the consequence of which was that many old shipmates emerged that I never thought I would hear from again, but of all the Jolly Jack Tars I had met only one has been seen and that was ex L/S Kemp of Scientology fame who appeared on the TV in some connection with that activity.

It is possibly just as well that contact is limited to correspondence for forty plus years does not lie lightly on many of us and we still like to think we are the same as those serious young men of eighteen and nineteen in the Heroic Days of the RN.

At the time, late 1944 when the RN was at the maximum for manpower, there were some 855,000 of us; 73,500 Wrns and the chaps totalling some 778,000, ten percent of whom would be officers so that leaves about 700,000 ratings; of those numbers some two thirds will now have journeyed on and those who survived the Great Adventure are in a minority.

For a time, until work dictated otherwise, I was involved with TS Deva, the Chester Sea Cadet Unit, housed appropriately enough in an old tea warehouse on what had once been the docks of the vanished Port of Chester.

My goodness, the RN had changed; Cutters and Whalers ? Well, yes,they had heard of them as last used during WW2; Seaman Manual and the creases in bell bottoms ? Never heard of it. Three stripes on the jean collar for Nelsons victories ?,Never heard of that either (incorrect anyway); still,salvation was at hand, bends and hitches were the same and the water was just as wet and the old uniform jumpers that you tore to bits getting them on and off have now been changed for something more sensible with zipps and of a better quality though still looking the same; the blue top winter issue caps have been scrapped in favour of white tops all year round and Pussers issue rum and hammocks a distant memory.

The strange status of Warrant Officer and the separate messing was finally resolved in 1948 when those remaining in the RN were made Sub-Lieutenants and moved to the Wardroom; however pressure from senior ratings in the service requested that an equivalent position to Warrant Officers in the Army and RAF be established in the RN for better equality of status, pay, pension rights and so forth *viz a viz* the other two services so a new senior rating was introduced called a Fleet Chief Petty Officer complete with new uniform badges; in the 1980's this rate was renamed Warrant Officer and is directly equivalent to Warrant Officers in the Army and RAF.

The Taxi driver uniforms of the Cooks, Supply, Stewards *et al* have been replaced with proper sailor's uniforms and the vast social and educational gulf between officers and ratings during my time has been reduced to more sensible proportions.

The technological revolution we spearheaded with our blood and thunder radar sets has now turned into a fully high tech. RN and Seamanship, once at a premium, has declined to the point where some ships do not have any such ratings at all.

In a couple of years time it will be fifty years since I joined the RN and it seems like yesterday; I am also thankful that I am still here to enjoy it, though very sadly many of my school friends and various contemporaries around the town did not have that good fortune (50,758 RN; 69,606 RAF and 144,079 Army died in the conflict) and many others suffer physical or psychological problems, many just starting to surface as a consequence of the pounding we all took.

Well, I still have my Pussers issue jack knife, shoe and clothes brushes and winter issue cap with a Bambara tally (it is an oval cap that replaced the round ones *circa* 1944), a medal to polish, a pile of photographs and, yes, a lot of memories.

BROADLANDS,
ROMSEY,
HAMPSHIRE.

26th March 1969.

Dear Mr. Lindop,

Thank you very much for your
letter of the 13th March.

I am so glad you and your
wife have enjoyed watching the T.V.
series of my life and times and
appreciate all the kind things you
say about the places and events
shown.

How interesting that you were
at the R.N.A.S. in Trincomalee in
1947.

Yours sincerely,

Mountbatten of Burma

NATIONAL MARITIME MUSEUM
From the Chairman of the Trustees
Admiral of the Fleet The Lord Lewin KG GCB LVO DSC

27 January 1990

Dear Mr. Lindop.

  I was very moved by your letter and thank you for responding to the appeal to covenant. I always like getting money from the Tax Man! As for Admirals, you should always remember that they are only Sub Lieutenants who have lived long and been lucky.

  Some of my wartime friends were Radar Operators – and indeed I married a WREN Radar Plotter 46 years ago. I was with the first radar in *Valiant* and the HO operators were strong supporters of the ships rugby XV, then later in the Tribal destroyer *Ashanti*, the Leading Hand in charge was an HO called Harry Scholes, a mature man who owned three dress shops in the Huddersfield area. He was a great steadying influence in the ship (by then I was the Jimmy, age 22) and he was awarded a well deserved DSM.

  I'm glad you have found the Museum of assistance with your research. We are not strong on WWII. Have you tried the Imperial War Museum? You will find them as helpful.

All good wishes

Yours sincerely

Terence Lewin

Ex-AB Lindop, J, D/JX 540875
Holly Bank
Duddon Common
Taporly CW6 0HG

Glossary and Abbreviations

ADCC   Air Defence Cadet Corps

ADDLS   Advanced Dummy Deck Landings - a marked off length of airfield runway used for trainee pilots prior to real carrier landings.

Admin   administration

ADR   Air Direction Room

AI   Admiralty Instructions

AI   radar beacon

Albacore a biplane manufactured by Fairey that replaced the Swordfish as a torpedo carrier.

AMC   Armed Merchant Cruiser

AP   Armour Piercing

Asdic   Active Sound Detection; today we call it Sonar - a method of locating submarines by their reflection of sound waves, the acoustic equivalent of radar. It was invented by the British at the end of World War 1 and by 1939 was fitted to most British destroyers and other vessels.

ASR   Air Sea Rescue

ASSW   Air and Surface Search and Warning

ATC   Air Training Corps

Avenger An aircraft of the US Navy manufactured by Grumman.

Barracuda An aircraft manufactured by Fairey and used by the Royal Navy during World War 2 as a carrier-borne torpedo bomber.

Beaufighter was an aircraft manufactured by the British Bristol Aeroplane Company and was a multi-role aircraft.

BHRS   Base Heavy Repair Ship

Bofors   a 40mm anti-aircraft gun manufactured by the Swedish Borfors Company. Guns manufactured by other companies of similar design were often called 'Bofors' in the same way that ball-point pens are sometimes called 'Biros'

C in C   Commander in Chief

CO   Commanding Officer

Corsair a carrier based aircraft used by the Fleet Air Arm.

CPO   Chief Pettty Officer

CRT	Cathode Ray Tube
CW	Commission and Warrant
Dakota	a transport aircraft
demob	demobilisation - a term denoting the end of military service.
DEMS	Defensively Equipped Merchant Ships
DH	De Haviland (UK Aircraft manufacturer)
dhoby	an Indian term for 'laundry'
DS	Depot Ship
ERA	Engine Room Artificer, a fitter, turner or boilermaker competent in the workings of engines and boilers
EVT	Educational and Vocational Training
Expeditor	a type of aircraft
FAA	Fleet Air Arm
FDO	Fighter Direction Officer
FDT	Fighter Direction Tender
Firefly	A carrier-born anti-submarine aircraft manufactured by Fairey.
FW Kondor	An all-metal four engined monoplane developed by Focke-Wulf. The Allies called the Kondor the KURIER
Garand	American semi-automatic rifle
GCI	Ground Controlled Interception
gen	general information
GL3	An Army radar.
Guzz	a slang term for The Naval base at Plymouth
HE	High Explosive
He 111	The Heinkel He 111 was a German aircraft
HF/DF	High Frequency Direction Finding
HMFDT	His Majesty's Fighter Direction Tender
HMLSF	His Majesty's Landing Ships Fighter Direction
HMS	His (Her) Majesty's Ship. A ship belonging to the Royal Navy
HQ	Headquarters
HRS	Heavy Repair Ship
H.O.	Hostilities Only
IWM	Imperial War Museum
i/c	in charge
Ju 88	The Junkers Ju 88 was a German multi-role combat aircraft.
KR	King's Regulations

Kriegsmarine   German Navy
KR&AI   King's Regulations and Admiralty Instructions
Lanchester sub-machine gun
Liberator An American heavy bomber designed by
            Consolidated Aircraft.
LSF   Landing Ships Fighter Direction
LSH(L)   Landing Ship HQ , the (L) is a code for converted
            from a civil merchantman
LST   Landing Ship Tank
Lt   Lieutenant
Luftwaffe German airforce
Luftflotte 3   Air Fleet 3. One of the many primary divisions of
            the German airforce
MADP   Main Air Display Plot
Martinets a type of aircraft
Master   a type of aircraft
Matloe   A sailor in the Royal Navy.
Mosquito a type of aircraft
MTB   Motor Torpedo Boat
m/cs   megacycles (radio frequency)
Natch   Natchykanda Camp
Nissen huts   are made from corregated metal and are
            approximately semi-circular in cross section.
NMM   National Maritime Museum
Oerlikon   a 20mm cannon used as both anti-aircraft and
            aircraft armament.
ops   operations
OTC   Office Training Corps
Pdr   pounder (describing a gun)
PO   Petty Officer
PPI   Plan Position Indicator
PRO   Public Records Office
PTI   Physical Training Instructor
Pusser   Pusser is a slang term for refering to the overall RN
            system and derives from Purser
Q Code was used in the days of Morse Code when a three
            letter designator would be transmitted and the
            translation made by referring to the Q Code Book.
QF   Quick Firer
QFE   Q Code for 'the atmospheric pressure of the
            aerodrome'
QNH   Q Code for 'the atmospheric pressure at sea level'

RA   Royal Arthur (The RN training establishment)
RAF   Royal Air Force
RC   Radar Control
RCM   Radio Countermeasures Office
RDF   Radio Direction Finder or Radio Direction Finding
RF   Radio-Frequency
RIN   Royal Indian Navy
RN   Royal Navy
RNAS   Royal Naval Air Station
RNB   Royal Naval Barracks
RNR   Royal Navy Reserve(s)
RNYE   RN Youth Entry
RP3   Radar Plotter 3rd Class
RPI   Radar Plotter Instructor
RTF   Radar Training Flotilla
RX   Reception of radio signal
R/T   Radio Telephone / Telephony
SBA   Sick Berth Attendant
Sea Otter a type of aircraft
Seafire An aircraft derived from the Spitfire it had folding wings
        for FAA carrier use..
SFCO   Senior Flying Control Officer
SS   Schutz-Staffel. A major paramilitary organisation under
        Adolf Hitler and the Nazi Party. In English it means
        Protection Squadron or defense corps.
SS   Steam Ship
Stuka   a Ju 87 dive bomber
sub   submarine
Swordfish A biplane designed by Fairey and used by the Fleet
        Air Arm as a torpedo bomber.
T5   Accoustic torpedo
Tiger Moth   A biplane designed by de Havilland and used
        extensively for training.
TX   Transmission of radio signal
Vengence   a type of aircraft
Very Light   A pyrotechnic signal fired from a special pistol. It
        used white or coloured balls.
VHF   Very High Frequency (radio channel designation)
VJ   Victory in Japan Day
WAAF   Women's Auxilliary Air Force

Walrus A biplane flying boat amphibian with a crew of three
manufactured by Westland and used for
reconnaissance work.
WO   Warrant Officer
WRNS Women's Royal Navy Service (Wrens)
WW1   World War One
WW2   World War Two
W/T   Wireless Telegraphy
York   a type of aircraft

The Publisher Says:

Phyllis Mary Lindop, (who John met whilst
doing some of the psychological and
educational papers to assess fitness for radar
training - see page 26), is the daughter of
Cecil Hearne Lindop and appears on Chart
9/5/1 of another Mercianotes publication.
John Barford Lindop is the son of William
Alfred Lindop and Sibley Barford Worral and
appears on Chart 9/6/1 of the same publication:

Nancy Lindop's Genealogies : Volume 1.

Published by Mercianotes

ISBN 9781905999217

Index

G

H

I

J

K

L

R

S

T

Printed in Great Britain
by Amazon

18501918R00088